THE GAMES OF CHILDREN

THE
GAMES OF CHILDREN
THEIR ORIGIN AND HISTORY

BY

HENRY BETT, M.A.

LONDON
METHUEN & CO. LTD.
1929

Now Reissued by
Singing Tree Press
1249 Washington Blvd., Detroit, Michigan 1968

First Published in 1929

Library of Congress Catalog Card Number 68–31218

TO

MY WIFE

1903–1928

PREFACE

THE kind reception given to my book on *Nursery Rhymes and Tales*, both by the Press and the public, has encouraged me to write the present study of a kindred subject, which was casually touched upon in the earlier volume.

Where I have proffered a conjecture of my own as to the origin of a game I have been careful to give sufficient evidence in corroboration, that the reader may judge for himself as to the validity of the explanation.

As before, whenever a foreign rhyme is quoted, I have given a doggerel translation of it, for the benefit of the general reader, and especially of children, who are usually much interested in the subject, as I have frequently observed.

CONTENTS

THE
GAMES OF CHILDREN

CHAPTER I

INTRODUCTORY

IT is generally known that many of our children's
games are old, but the extreme antiquity of
some of them is not often realized. Those who
are familiar with the older literature of our own
land, or with the classical literature of Greece and
Rome, will have noticed references to familiar games
which show that some of them were played hundreds
of years and some of them thousands of years ago.
This is almost trivial when set beside the prehistoric
origin of many games, but it is interesting enough
in its way.

Thus, to give a few examples almost at random,
there are numerous references in the Greek and
Latin poets to games played with balls, hoops, and
tops. Homer gives us a delightful picture of the
white-armed Nausicaa and her maidens playing at
ball.[1] The exiled Ovid, when his thoughts turn
homeward in the spring, remembers that in Rome
the children will now be playing with balls and
hoops :

Nunc pila, nunc celeri volvitur orbe trochus.

(Now flies the ball, now rolls the whirling hoop.)[2]

The latter pastime cannot have been confined to mere children, for Horace laments that the degenerate Roman youth neglected the manlier sports of riding and hunting :

—ludere doctior
Seu Graeco iubeas trocho,
Seu malis vetita legibus alea.[3]

('being better skilled
To guide the Greek hoop on its rapid way,
Or with the dice, by law forbid, to play.')

Callimachus describes 'the boys at the wide cross-roads whipping their swift tops' (θοὰς βέμβικας),[4] and tells how the words spoken in their sport were taken as an omen. Virgil, depicting the frenzy of Amata, says that she raged through the city :

Ceu quondam torto volitans sub verbere turbo,
Quem pueri magno in gyro vacua atria circum
Intenti ludo exercent.[5]

('As sometimes boys, intent upon their sport,
With twisted lash drive round some empty court
The whirling top.')

But probably the most interesting allusion to a child's game in any ancient writer is in a passage in Petronius, where he describes how a boy climbed on to the back of Trimalchio 'and slapped him on the shoulders with his hand, laughing and calling out, *Bucca, bucca, quot sunt hic ?*'[6] This is precisely the same game, and, what is more extraordinary, played with precisely the same formula, as that played by English schoolboys to-day, where a boy 'sets a back' and other boys leap on to it, holding up so many fingers, with the cry, 'Buck, buck, how many horns do I hold up ?'

Some interesting references to children's games are found also in mediaeval writers. There is a familiar game in which a flower is used as an oracle. The petals are stripped off one by one with the formula, ' He loves me, he loves me not ! ' This game has several forms, for it may be played with a stalk of grass, or by counting the pips or kernels of fruit, and with words which indicate your future social status, ' Tinker, tailor, soldier, sailor, rich man, poor man, beggarman, thief ! '⁷ or which refer to the date of your marriage, ' This year, next year, sometime, never ! ' or to the kind of house in which you are to live after that happy event, ' Big house, little house, pigsty, barn ! '⁸ This kind of oracle is described in the twelfth century by Walther von der Vogelweide, the greatest of the German minnesingers :

> Mich hât ein halm gemachet frô :
> er giht, ich süle genâde vinden.
> ich maz daz selbe kleine strô,
> als ich hie vore sach von kinden.
> nû hoeret unde merket, ob si'z denne tuo :
> " si tuot, si entuot, si tuot, si entuot, si tuot ".⁹

> (This flower stalk shall my fate decide,
> And tell if happily I woo ;
> I strip it down, from side to side,
> As I have seen the children do :
> Now mark—what does it bode of good or ill ?—
> " She will, she won't, she will, she won't, *she will* ".)

It may be added that there is another reference to this practice in a great German poet of later days, for Goethe makes Margaret keep Faust waiting while she plucks a flower, and strips off the leaves, saying : ' He loves me—He loves me not—

He loves me—Not—He loves me—Not—He loves me ! '[10]

Then there are references to children's games also in writers of the Renaissance. Thus Rabelais tells us that Gargantua, in his amazing childhood, played with his companions at many games, among them those which he calls *A mariage, A je te pince sans rire, A cligne-musette, A je vous prends sans vert, Aux ponts chus.*[11] The first was evidently a wedding game of the type of *Sally Waters* ; the second was something like the game of *Buff*, where you have to refrain from smiling when provoked to it ; the third was the equivalent of our *Blindman's Buff* ; the fourth was a game in which a green leaf was worn, as in the American game of *Green !* or our ritual for Royal Oak Day ; and the fifth was a game like *London Bridge is Broken Down.*

There are numerous allusions to children's games in our own Elizabethan writers. The game mentioned a moment ago as *Blindman's Buff* used to be called *Hoodman Blind.* When every one wore a hood the simplest way of blindfolding a person was to reverse his hood so as to cover his face.[12] Hamlet says to his mother :

> ‘ What devil was't
> That thus hath cozen'd you at hoodman blind ? ’[13]

When Parolles is blindfolded one of the lords exclaims : ‘ Hoodman comes ! ’[14] In the sixteenth-century French dictionary of Cotgrave *Clignemusset* is defined as ‘ the childish play called Hodman blind, Harrie-racket, or are you all hid.’ The game of *Barley-break*, very popular in those days, is referred to several times by Sidney in his *Arcadia.*

It appears to have been a game of the type of *Prisoner's Base*, played by couples on ground marked out into three compartments, the middle one being known as ' Hell '. The couple in this compartment had to try to catch the others as they advanced toward it ; if successful in this, the couples changed places. When the game ended (as when it began) one pair of players was necessarily in what boys call ' the den ' ; hence the other name of the pastime, *The Last Couple in Hell*,[15] as in Herrick's poem *Barley-Break, or Last in Hell* :

> ' We two are last in Hell : what may we feare
> To be tormented or kept pris'ners here ?
> Alas ! if kissing be of plagues the worst
> We'll wish in Hell we had been last and first.'[16]

Apart from literature altogether, there are interesting points of connexion between some of our games and the historic usages of the past. Thus there is a singular relation between one detail in the game of cricket and the ancient methods of agriculture. The land used to be cultivated in long strips divided by balks of unploughed turf. Where the eight-oxen plough was used a long furrow was a necessity, and the width of the strip of ground was proportionately lessened. We derive several measures from the size and shape of this strip. The acre was not in its origin merely a measure of ground ; it was a unit of cultivation. The earliest English law that fixed the size of the statute acre (in the reign of Edward I) declared that ' forty perches in length and four in breadth make an acre '.[17] That is to say, the acre was a strip two hundred and twenty yards long (hence our ' furlong ', which means 'a furrow-long') and twenty-two yards wide. Now, when the villagers played on the stubbles it was natural to choose an acre-strip to throw their ball across from balk to balk, and that is why the cricket-pitch to-day is twenty-two yards.[18]

Another game is related to the ancient custom of 'beating the bounds '. This rite was observed on one of the three days before Ascension Day. The clergyman and the churchwardens, accompanied by the parishioners, went round the boundaries of the parish in solemn procession. Naogeorgus describes the ceremony :

'Now comes the day wherein they gad abrode, with Crosse
    in hande,
To boundes of every field, and round about their neigh-
    bour's lande :
And as they go, they sing and pray to euery saint aboue,
But to our Lady specially, whom most of all they loue.
Whenas they to the towne are come, the Church they enter
    in,
And look what Saint that Church doth guide, they humbly
    pray to him,
That he preserve both corne and fruite from storm and
    tempest great,
And them defend from harme, and send them store of
    drink and meat.'[19]

Thus the rite had a religious aspect, but the real purpose of it was to maintain in memory the proper boundaries of the parish, with its landmarks. Naturally these last were often trees. Thus at Basingstoke the perambulation always began from the spot where a great elm used to stand at the junction of three roads.[20] The boundaries of the township of Wolverhampton in time past were marked at several points by what were called

' Gospel Trees ', because during the annual perambulation the clergyman read a passage from the
Gospels there.[21]
On the occasion of these perambulations boys
were made to stand upon their heads in holes dug
in the ground, or forced to jump wide brooks, into
which they fell, or thrown into a bed of nettles, or
soundly beaten, when they came to particular
places, so that they should remember those exact
spots all their life.[22] There is an item in the
Churchwardens' Books of Chelsea, relating to the
perambulation of the bounds in 1679, ' Given to
the boys that were whipt, four shillings.'[23] There
cannot be much doubt that we have an imitation
of ' beating the bounds ' in the processional game
which is played with the formula :

> ' Round and round the village,
> Round and round the village,
> Round and round the village,
> As we have done before ! '[24]

But the references to children's games in the
literature of the past, and the relations between
them and the customs of historical times, become
insignificant in comparison with the prehistoric
sources of these games. The very remote origin of
many children's games is probably seldom realized,
except by the professed student of primitive culture.
It would be natural to suppose that the games
which children play were merely invented, either
by children themselves or by adults for the benefit
of children ; and that, of course, may be true of
some games. But it is beyond doubt that most
games are not inventions at all, but imitations—

imitations on the part of children of the life of their elders. Nothing is more characteristic of the child than this faculty of imitation. The girl with her doll imitates a mother with a baby, the boy with his rocking-horse imitates a man on horseback, a troop of lads with sticks for swords and a battered can for a drum imitate a company of soldiers, and so on. But the striking fact is that in many instances the imitation dates back to the life of prehistoric times. So that the real interest for the student of folk-lore is in those games which still reflect, more or less plainly, some feature of primitive life. It is also to be remembered that games of various kinds had a place in the life of adults in early times (as they have in savage lands to this day), and indeed possessed a religious significance, as the games of classical antiquity are alone enough to remind us. So among the Red Indians to-day it is stated that the games of the adults generally are played ceremonially, as pleasing to the gods, and with the purpose of securing fertility, causing rain, expelling demons, and so on.[25] It is quite likely that the children in prehistoric times imitated these sacred games, as they imitated all the other doings of their elders, so that it is possible that some children's games are the ghosts of these ancient mysteries.

One of the principal difficulties in treating of children's games is the considerable mixture of types. Different games, based upon a different range of conceptions, present similarities of detail. It is easy enough to detect the primitive meaning here and there, but very often a game of one particular type has become approximated to a game of another type altogether, and the result is a mixture of motive. It may be that in one example both motives are plainly present, while in another example one of them has been somewhat obscured. Thus games of the type of *Oats and Beans and Barley Grow*, which undoubtedly have arisen from the magic rites intended to promote the growth of the crops, are often approximated to games like *Sally Waters*, which are an imitation of marriage. It may be suggested that there really was a connexion between the two motives, by way of the primitive notion of fecundity, but it is more likely that one game in practice has simply blended with another, and borrowed some part of its action and its formula.

It is only by the patient comparison of children's games of various types as they exist in different lands with one another, with all sorts of superstitious survivals in civilized countries, and with existing practices among savage peoples, that the primitive significance of them can be established. Nothing can exhibit the amazing tenacity of popular tradition more clearly than the relics of prehistoric belief and custom which are fossilized in the games that are played by children, generation after generation.

CHAPTER II

WEDDINGS AND FUNERALS

IT has been said already that many children's games are obviously imitations of events which recur in the life of adults around them. Now, the most impressive of these events, as far as the ritual and the spectacular aspect are concerned, are the occasions of marriage and of burial. Consequently these are quite plainly reflected in games. It is recorded that our Lord said, when He complained that the men of his day would not accept either His friendly mission or the sterner witness of John the Baptist : 'But whereunto shall I liken this generation ? It is like unto children sitting in the market-place, and calling unto their fellows, and saying, We have piped unto you, and ye have not danced ; we have mourned unto you, and ye have not lamented.'[26] These children, in other words, had attempted to play at weddings, and then at funerals, and some of their perverse playmates would not join in either sort of game. Ever since those days the children have continued to play at marriages and burials, as they had done for ages before our Lord saw them doing it in the streets of Nazareth.

Later on we shall discover several traces of prehistoric custom in games which imitate a betrothal and a wedding. But first of all we may note that many games turn upon the action of

choosing a bride. Thus in one English game a
number of children stand in a row, and two other
children advance toward them hand in hand, saying :

> ' Stepping up the green grass,
>   Thus, and thus, and thus,
> Will you let one of your fair maids
>   Come and play with us ?
> We will give you pots and pans,
>   We will give you brass,
> We will give you anything
>   For a pretty lass ! '

Upon receiving a refusal, they repeat the first
quatrain, and add :

> ' We will give you gold and silver,
>   We will give you pearl,
> We will give you anything
>   For a pretty girl ! '

This time consent is given, and the two lead out a
girl from the row, and dance round her singing :

> ' Come, my dearest (*the girl's name*),
>   Come and play with us,
> You shall have a young man
>   Born for your sake.
> And the bells shall ring,
> And the birds shall sing,
> And we'll all clap hands together.'

It is significant that the last part of the ritual is
expressly called ' the wedding '.[27]

So in another widespread game :

> ' Here come three knights out of Spain
>   A-courting of your daughter Jane.'

> ' My daughter Jane she is too young,
>   She can't abide a flattering tongue.'

After some parleying the knights are bidden :

> ' Walk up the kitchen and down the hall,
> And choose the fairest of them all.'

Then the choice is made :

> ' Madam, to you I bow and bend,
> I take you for my dearest friend.'

Or, in some versions :

> ' The fairest one that I can see
> Is pretty (*a girl's name*). Come to me ! '[28]

There are many games like these, quite plainly based on the ritual of marriage. A boy chooses a girl, or a girl a boy, and the accompanying rhyme is all concerned with the choice and the marriage, as in the game of *Sally Waters* :

> ' Sally, Sally Waters, come sprinkle in your pan,
> For down in the meadows there lies a young man,
> Rise, Sally ! rise, Sally !
> And don't you look sad,
> For you shall have a husband, good or bad,
> Choose you east, choose you west,
> Choose the one that you love best.
>
> Now you're married we wish you joy,
> First a girl and then a boy,
> Seven years now, and seven to come,
> Take her and kiss her, and send her off home.'[29]

It is noticeable that in nearly all the numerous variants of the game that have been collected there is the reference to water—' sprinkle in the pan ', or ' water with the can ', or some such phrase. In some versions there are other references to water :

> ' And now you're married, I wish you joy,
> First a girl and then a boy ;

Seven years after son and daughter,
And now, young people, jump over the water !

In other versions the last line is :

' Kiss each other and come out of the water ! '[30]

On the strength of these allusions to water, and the name of the girl in the game, an attempt has been made to connect *Sally Waters* with *Sul*, a goddess of the waters worshipped at Bath, where there was a Roman temple dedicated to Sulis-Minerva. There was a place in Brittany known in Roman times as Sulis, and it was probably identical with the present St. Anne d'Auray, which is famed for its waters.[31] The conjecture as to the connexion with *Sul* is the less convincing because there is evidence as to sprinkling with water being a part of the marriage rite in various lands. The bride in ancient Rome was sprinkled with water. In Esthonia on the morning after the wedding the bride throws into the spring offerings to the water-spirit, and then sprinkles the bridegroom with water.[32] Among the Mundas in Bengal a pitcher of water is poured over the bride and bridegroom.[33] In Albania the bride's mother sprinkles the bridegroom with water when he arrives at her house. The Turkish bridegroom, on proceeding to the women's apartments to see his bride for the first time, upsets a bowl of water on the stairs and scatters it in all directions. In Russia the parents of the bride and bridegroom are soused with water.[34]

There are marriage games, more or less similar, in other lands. Rabelais records that Gargantua and his comrades played the game *A Mariage*.

French children still play at *Les Mariages*, and the formula is, in one version :

> ' Eh ! qui marierons-nous ? eh ! qui marierons-nous ?
> Mademoiselle, ce sera vous ! '

whereupon a girl is chosen. Then she is bidden :

> ' Entrez dans la danse ! '

Then the chant proceeds :

> ' J'aimerai qui m'aimera, j'aimerai qui m'aime.'

Then :

> ' Eh ! qui lui donnerons-nous ? eh ! qui lui donnerons-
> nous ? '

and the answer is :

> ' Mon beau monsieur, ce sera vous ! '

Then the players repeat :

> ' J'aimerai qui m'aimera, j'aimera qui m'aime.'

And then the action ends with :

> ' Amants, embrassez-vous, amants, embrassez-vous ! '[35]

> (' Whom shall I marry ? whom shall I marry ?
> Tell us, do—
> Mademoiselle, you !
> I will love the one who loves me best, and I love you.

> Whom shall I have ? whom shall I have ?
> Tell us, do—
> Monsieur, you !
> I will love the one who loves me best, and I love you.
> Embrace each other, lovers, now ! ')

Another French marriage game, which strikes one as sophisticated, has the rhyme :

Je suis envoyé de Cythère
Pour marier tous les amants ;
Sans contrat, ni sans notaire,
Je les unis à l'instant.
Si vous aimez le mariage
Entrez dans le rond, et choisissez ! '

Here a boy and a girl pair off in the dance, and
the rhyme ends :

' Donnez un baiser pour gage
Et le contrat sera passé.'[36]

(' Venus has sent me here with speed
    To marry each true lover ;
Of priest and book there is no need,
    The rite is quickly over.
For wedded life you need a wife,
    So come, and do not linger,
Give her a kiss to seal your bliss ;
    The ring is on your finger ! ')

Apart from the references to water in the game
of *Sally Waters* there has been nothing in these
marriage games so far to suggest anything particularly ancient, for the allusions to the wedding feast
and the wedding-bells which sometimes occur are
natural enough and modern enough. But it is
significant that in some games there is *an allusion
to catching and carrying off the bride*. Thus in one
English game the principal action is for a boy to
seize a girl, and the material part of the rhyme is :

' (*A girl's name*) with her rosy cheeks
    Catch her if you can,
And if you cannot catch her
    I'll tell you who's the man.

(*A girl's name*) made a pudding,
    She made it very sweet,

She daren't stick a knife in
    Till (*a boy's name*) came home at neet.

Taste (*a boy's name*), taste, and don't say Nay !
    Perhaps to-morrow morning'll be our wedding day.
The bells shall ring, and we shall sing,
    And all clap hands together ! '[37]

In the game of *Drop Handkerchief* (which used to be played in Devonshire especially at Easter and Whitsun) the girl is pursued and seized.[38] In the other familiar game *Here We Come Gathering Nuts in May*, there is no obvious element of courtship, but there is a struggle for the possession of an individual, and it is *a boy* who drags away *a girl*, with the formula :

' Here we come gathering nuts in May,
    Nuts in May, nuts in May ;
Here we come gathering nuts in May,
    On a cold and frosty morning.'

' And who have you come to gather away,
    To gather away, to gather away,
And who have you come to gather away
    On a cold and frosty morning ? '

' We have come to gather (*a girl's name*) away,
    On a cold and frosty morning.'

' And who will you send to fetch her away,
    On a cold and frosty morning ? '

' We'll send (*a boy's name*) to fetch her away
    On a cold and frosty morning.'[39]

To this extent, therefore, it belongs to the general type of game where some one seizes a bride.

Now the seizure of a bride at once brings to mind some remarkable traditions which have come down to us from the early life of man. Thus there is a striking story in the Old Testament of the men of

Benjamin carrying off the daughters of Shiloh.[40]
The chronicler describes this as a prearranged
method of avoiding the breach of an oath, but that
is evidently a rationalization of a very old tradition
—the tale of how one tribe had got wives by carrying
off women of another tribe. Again, one of the most
famous of the legends of early Rome is that of the
Rape of the Sabines. The story is that when
Romulus built the city, in order to people it he
made it a place of sanctuary for those who had shed
blood, and runaway slaves, and the like. The
result was that the inhabitants of the neighbouring
cities would not give their daughters in marriage to
such disreputable settlers. To remedy this Romulus
devised an unscrupulous plot. He invited the
Sabines and the people of the neighbouring towns
to witness the Consualia—the games in honour of
the god Consus. While the visitors were intent
upon the spectacle, the Roman youths rushed in
and seized all the marriageable maidens. These
were soon reconciled to their strange lot, but their
kinsfolk determined to avenge the outrage, and a
war was the result, in which Romulus and the
Romans were victorious. This, again, is one of the
numerous instances in which a legend has grown
up to account for an early usage the original character of which had been forgotten. There are
other ancient examples where there has been no
rationalizing legend at all, but where the fact is
baldly stated. So Plutarch, when he is narrating
the life of Lycurgus, and incidentally describing the
customs of Sparta, tells us that in the Spartan
marriages the husband carried off his bride ' by a
sort of force ' (δι' ἁρπαγῆς).[41]

Such stories as these, with the many parallels which exist in savage life, and some legal survivals, set modern ethnologists on to the study of the whole subject of primitive marriage. The broad result has been to establish the fact that one of the most widespread practices of primitive people is the usage which has been named exogamy—the custom of marrying out of the clan. It was explained by one of the earlier authorities as the result of female infanticide. It has been a common practice among savage peoples to kill off the girls in infancy. They are no good for hunting or for fighting, and yet they must be fed if they are kept, and so they are simply killed off while they are babies. Hence a scarcity of women, which, it was argued, led to polyandry within the tribe, and to the capture of women from outside. It is more probable, however, that the main reason for exogamy is to be found in the fact that in a very early stage of human society the women of the tribe were common property, and no man had a right to appropriate a woman for himself. But if he captured a woman from another tribe the position was different. She was his very own, the captive of his sword and of his bow, and no other man had any right to her. Many things would help forward the practice of exogamy, when once it had begun. The scarcity of women resulting from the infanticide of girls, the evil results of continued intermarriage within the tribe, the natural desire on the part of both the man and the woman to possess each other exclusively, and the inevitable increase, both in numbers and in the physical strength of individuals, of exogamous tribes, would all tend to make the usage prevail in the course of time. It was once widespread in the world, perhaps almost universal. It still exists amongst various tribes in Africa, America, Australia, and India.

Thus in Australia the natives are divided into great families, all the members of a family bearing the same name. These names are common over a large part of the continent, and 'a man cannot marry a woman of his own family name'. Very often the practice is linked up with totemism.[42] The Tsimheean Indians in British Columbia are divided into totem-clans, and the relationship within these is closer than that within the tribe. The totems are the whale, the porpoise, the eagle, the coon, the wolf, and the frog. Members of the same tribe may marry, but not if they both have the same totem ; a whale may not marry a whale, but a whale may marry a frog, and so forth. Evidently the prohibition does not always connect with the totem, except as the totem is a sign of relationship, for among the Omaha Indians, where the same kind of prohibition prevails, a man may marry a woman of his own totem, provided she is a member of another tribe.[43] The Chinese people is divided into a number of clans each distinguished by a name borne by all its members. The number of these names is limited—it has been put as low as a hundred and as high as a thousand.[44] A man may not marry a woman of his own clan name.[45] Similarly the Indians of Guiana are divided into families, each with a distinct name—the Siwidi, the Karuafudi, the Onisidi, and so on. No one is allowed to marry a person bearing the same family name.[46] In India it is unlawful for a Brahman to marry a wife whose clan name or *gotra* is the same

as his own.[47] So a Kalmuck can only marry a
woman from another horde, and a Jakut can only
marry a woman from another clan.[48] Among the
Kaffirs marriage between people of the same family
name is absolutely prohibited.[49] The Togo in West
Africa hold that marriage within the same clan is
incest ; when it occurs the dreadful crime causes a
drought.[50] Some of the Tartars hold it a sin for
two persons of the same family name to marry, so
that a man must not take a wife of his own tribe.[51]
It is possible that there is a survival of this ancient
prejudice in the dislike which exists still in some
parts of England for a marriage between parties of
the same name, and in the proverb about marriage :

> Change the name and not the letter,
> Change for worse and not for better.

In many ways exogamy has left traces upon
marriage customs. There are regions where the
actual seizure of a bride by force still occurs. Thus
it is stated that among the Kols of the north-east
of India a young man will seize a girl in the public
market, and, assisted by a party of his friends, will
carry her off, struggling and screaming, without any
interference on the part of those who look on, unless
they happen to be her relatives, and the friends of
the girl are apt to admire and applaud the feat.[52]

In many cases, however, the seizure has become
merely formal—a traditional part of the marriage
ceremonies. The pretence of capture and the
pretence of resistance is kept up, more or less
realistically, but there is a preliminary under-
standing between the parties, and it is all a part
of the wedding ritual. It is interesting to note the

different ways in which it is carried out, varying
from an uncomfortable degree of realism to pure
formality.   Thus in some parts of New Guinea,
when a man takes a wife from the mountains he is
said to *steal* her, and in the past he used to be shot
at with arrows as he carried her off.[53]   The imitative
rite prevails among the Khonds, in the hilly regions
of Orissa, and a British officer has left a vivid
description of the bridegroom making off as fast as
he can, carrying upon his back a bundle swathed
with scarlet cloth, which is really the bride, and
surrounded by a bodyguard of a score or more
young men, while desperate attacks are made upon
the party by a crowd of young women, who hurl
stones and bamboos at the bridegroom's head.[54]
Among the Moluches of southern Chili the bride is
carried off by pretended violence, and this is considered an essential prerequisite to the nuptials.
The prospective husband (though he has an agreement beforehand with the girl's father) conceals
himself, accompanied by some friends, where he
knows the girl is likely to pass.   Then she is seized,
and carried off on horseback behind the bridegroom,
despite her shrieks and resistance, which are nothing
but pretence.[55]   So among the natives of Tierra del
Fuego, though the bridegroom has previously gained
the consent of the bride's parents, he must build or
borrow a canoe, watch his opportunity, and then
carry off his bride.[56]

Sometimes the practice has become reduced to a
show of force by the bridegroom in rending the
bride's clothes, or a show of reluctance on the part
of the bride in escaping from the bridegroom.
Thus among the Tunguzes the bridegroom must

overcome the bride by force, and tear her clothes in the struggle.[57] It is the custom among the Koryak for the bride's clothes to be tied up, and for her to attempt to run away from the bridegroom. He pursues her, and cuts her garments loose.[58] The Mantras of the Malay Peninsula on the wedding-day give the bride a start, and then the bridegroom must either catch her or forfeit her.[59] Among the Bedouin of Sinai if the girl gets any inkling of her betrothal she makes a show of escaping to the mountains ; in one tribe it seems that she does actually hide herself in the mountains for three days.[60]

Some of these customs survived in our own islands until modern times. Actual bride-capture appears to have been practised in Ireland in some cases as late as 1767.[61] The pretence of it survived later still. A writer on life in Northern Ireland, early in the nineteenth century, after describing the marriage customs among the Ulster folk of Scottish descent, proceeds : ' The Irish Wedding is somewhat different, especially in the mountainous districts. However suitable the match, it is but a lame exploit, and even an affront, *if the groom does not first run away with the bride.* After a few days' carousal among the groom's friends, the weddingers move toward the bride's country, on which occasion not only every relative, but every poor fellow who aspires to be the well-wisher of either party, doth bring with him a bottle of whisky, or the price of a bottle, to the rendezvous. After this second edition of matrimonial hilarity, the bride and groom proceed quietly to their designed home.'[62]

An earlier account of marriage customs in Ireland, dating from about 1682, states that ' the parents and friends on each side meet on the side of a hill, or if the weather be cold, in some place of shelter about midway between both dwellings. If agreement ensue, they drink the *Agreement Bottle*, as they call it, which is a bottle of good Usquebaugh, and this goes merrily around. For payment of the portion, which generally is a determinate number of cows, little care is taken. . . . On the day of bringing home, the bridegroom and his friends ride out, and meet the bride and her friends at the place of treaty. Being come near each other, *the custom was of old to cast short darts at the company that attended the bride,* but at such a distance that seldom any hurt ensued ; yet it is not out of memory of man that the Lord Hoath on such an occasion lost an eye : this custom of casting darts is now obsolete.'[63] The usage survived also in Wales. Lord Kames has left it on record as still happening in the early years of the nineteenth century. On the morning of the wedding day the bridegroom went on horseback, accompanied by his friends, to the bride's home, and demanded his bride. Her friends, also mounted on horseback in readiness, refused the demand. Then a mock fight ensued, during which *the bride was carried off,* mounted behind her nearest kinsman, and pursued by the bridegroom and his friends. After a time they were allowed to overtake and capture her, and the bridegroom led her off in triumph. The day concluded with a feast.[64]

It has been suggested that the throwing of old shoes after a wedding party is a relic of throwing missiles at the party that carried off the bride,[65] and that the very name of ' best man ' is derived from that of the 'best men'[66]—the boldest and bravest of the bridegroom's friends—who were his bodyguard on the nuptial raid. There is some evidence, however, that it has been a custom to fling old shoes after your friends as a token of good luck, not only at weddings, but at the start of other enterprises—when servants were going to a new place, or when sailors were going on a fresh voyage, for example.[67] It is possible that the usage was first a marriage custom, and that then, when the original meaning of it was forgotten, it was interpreted in terms of the good wishes that were general at weddings, and finally extended in that sense to other occasions. It does not appear ever to have been anything like as general at any other time as at weddings, which would rather suggest an extension from the occasion of marriages to other occasions when good wishes were natural. So the poet says without any nuptial reference :

> 'And wheresoe'er you move, good luck
> Shall fling her old shoe after.' [68]

Several of the children's games which we have quoted, where there is a seizure or a pursuit of the bride, probably go back to the primitive marriage by capture. It is significant to read that among Australian tribes where it was the usual custom for the men to get wives by carrying them off by violence from other tribes, one of the regular games of the native children was *to play at this kind of capture.*[69]

It is only fair to say that some anthropologists in these days explain many of the rites accompanying marriage rather as magical ceremonies than as survivals of bride-capture. A wedding is a *rite de passage*, and to enter into a new condition or indeed to do anything for the first time is always considered as attended with supernatural dangers. This is all the more so in a marriage, because the primitive mind regards sexual intercourse as a mysterious and perilous thing. Hence some recent authorities regard many practices such as carrying the bride and throwing missiles after her as prophylactic and propitiatory ceremonies.[70] For example, the bride in Morocco is pelted with stones when she leaves her old home—an obvious parallel to the throwing of an old shoe in England—but the explanation given was, sometimes, that it was done ' to rid her of her evil ', and sometimes that it was done ' to cause her to take her evil with her '. [71]

The last relic of primitive wedding ceremonies in our own land (apart from children's games) is probably the custom of lifting the bride over the threshold of her new home after the wedding.[72] This has survived as a marriage custom in many lands in Europe, as well as in Egypt, Palestine, and China.[73] It was once a universal custom in our own country. There is a reference to it in Herrick's *Epithalamium to Sir Thomas Southwell and his Lady* :

> ' You, you that be of her nearest kin,
> *Now o'er the threshold force her in.*
>   But, to avert the worst
>   Let her her fillets first
>   Knit to the posts ; this point
>   Remembering, to anoint
>   The sides, for 'tis a charm
>   Strong against future harm,[74]
> And the evil deeds the which
> There was hidden by the witch.'

Sir Walter Scott states, in a note to *Guy Mannering*, that the custom of lifting a bride over the threshold prevailed in Scotland at the time when he wrote. He connects it with the other custom of setting the door ajar when anyone is dying.[75] ' And wha ever heard of a door being barred when a man was in the dead-thraw ? ' said Meg Merrilies ; ' how d'ye think the spirit was to get awa' through bolts and bars like thae ? ' Scott suggests that both usages are due to the sanctity of the threshold, which was ' in some sort a sacred limit, and the subject of much superstition '.[76] It is probable that the opening of the door at the moment of death is not connected with the sanctity of the threshold, but rather with the notion of making a ready way of escape for the departing spirit. A locked or closed door would hinder the exit of the soul.[77]

So there is a widespread custom of unlocking and opening doors while a birth is taking place. It still survives in Germany ; and it did survive, not so long ago, in Scotland. The usage has been recorded in many parts of the world. Obviously it connects with the similar customs of untying knots,[78] loosening plaits of hair and shoe-laces, opening boxes, and even unfastening moored boats and tethered cattle at a similar time. The underlying notion is that anything shut or fast will hinder birth.[79]

It is true enough that the threshold was sacred, and there is a great deal of curious evidence of it, ranging from early Rome, where the plough that traced the furrow which was to be the line of a newly founded city's walls had to be lifted over the places where the gates were to be built,[80] to modern Tartary, where it is still an offence, as we know it was six centuries ago, to tread on the threshold on entering a tent.[81]   Marco Polo relates that two men armed with staves guarded the entrance of the audience hall of the Khan of Tartary expressly to prevent anyone stepping on the threshold.[82] The sanctity of the threshold may quite possibly have had something to do with the lifting of the bride.[83]

So may the fear of stumbling.   There is a widespread notion that to stumble at the beginning of any enterprise is an evil omen.[84]   It was thought a presage of ill fortune when Caesar stumbled at landing on the coast of Africa, but ' he averted the evil omen with happy presence of mind, looking at the handful of soil he had grasped in his fall, and exclaiming, " Africa, thou art mine ! " ' [85]   Precisely the same story is told of the landing of William the Conqueror in England.   He stumbled, and some of his lords said, ' This is a bad sign ! '   ' What is the matter ? ' said William.   ' What astonishes you ?   I have grasped this land with my hands, and, by the splendour of God, how far soever it may extend, it is mine, it is yours ! ' [86]   It is curious that this superstition about stumbling has been justified by modern psychologists.   Freud has pointed out that it really depends upon the fact that stumbling results from the nervous inhibition which is the physical expression of fear, so that it is likely enough that some repressed fear or anxiety about an enterprise, which will quite probably make the ultimate result of it unfortunate, may express itself in stumbling on setting out upon it.[87]   It would be easier to stumble at a threshold than anywhere else, so that it may perhaps have been a desire to avoid this evil omen that helped to keep up the practice of lifting the bride over the threshold.

But we cannot think that the lifting of the bride over the threshold is altogether unconnected with marriage by capture. Plutarch suggests that the custom in Rome was probably ' in remembrance of those first wives whom they ravished perforce from the Sabines ',[88] and there may be an actual tradition of the origin behind his remark. There is some evidence that can scarcely be explained either by the sanctity of the threshold or by the fear of stumbling on it, or even, in every case, as a propitiatory rite. Among the Bedouin the bridegroom uses force to make the bride enter his tent, where the emphasis of the rite is not upon the detail of the threshold at all, but upon the compulsory character of the entry.[89] So among the Hausa the bride is brought to the bridegroom's house, and his friends try to get her to enter, but she refuses. Then money is given to the bridesmaids who have accompanied her and they pull and push her in.[90] Here again the stress is evidently on the enforced entry, and there is no mention of the threshold. And in Friesland it is significant that the lifting has no reference whatever to the threshold, but the relic of primitive custom remains in the ' bride-lifter ' who lifts the bride and her bridesmaid into the wagon.[91] The custom of lifting the bride still survives. There was a photograph in a London newspaper in the year 1927 of Lord Inverclyde carrying his bride over the threshold on their arrival at Castle Wemyss after the wedding.

There is perhaps still another trace of primitive custom in relation to marriages in our children's

games. The game of *Kiss in the Ring* is obviously
a marriage game. In the game of *Drop Handkerchief*, which is practically a variant of it, a girl drops
a handkerchief in front of a boy, who then chases
and captures her. Both games are played with
some such formula as :

' I sent a letter to my love,
And on the way I dropped it, dropped it, dropped it,
And on the way I dropped it ! '

Now, in the game of *Queen Anne*,[92] which is of
the same type as these last, three girls are disguised
so as to appear alike, and the leader of the game
brings them to a boy with the words :

' Come, choose your own ; come, choose from all ! '

whereupon he has to guess the right one. It is
possible that this is a relic of another detail in
primitive marriage. For there is a curious custom,
found in many lands, by which the bride is placed
among several other women, veiled or dressed
exactly alike. So at Fez in Morocco the bride is
accompanied by half a dozen or more female relatives who are dressed like her, so that no one can
distinguish between them : this is said to be to
protect her from magic and the evil eye.[93]   In
some countries the bridegroom has to pick out the
bride from among her companions when all are
veiled, or hidden behind a curtain, or dressed so as
to be confusingly alike. There are many folk-tales
which turn upon this. Sometimes it is some
physical peculiarity, such as the loss of a finger or
a toe, that leads to recognition. Sometimes the
bride arranges to help the bridegroom by giving

him some secret token, such as a wink, at the critical moment. Sometimes a friendly animal gives him a sign, as when an insect which has promised to help alights on the bride's face. So in the German folk-tale Simpleton has to choose among the three sleeping daughters of the king, who are all exactly alike, the one who is youngest. They had eaten different sweetmeats before falling asleep —one some sugar, one some syrup, and the youngest some honey. So the queen of the bees, that Simpleton had befriended, came and tasted their lips, and then settled on the mouth of the one who had eaten the honey.[94]

The custom of making the bridegroom choose amongst several pretending brides actually survives. At peasant weddings in Lorraine the bride and three other girls are dressed alike so as to make recognition difficult. If the bridegroom guesses right at first he dances with his bride all the evening ; if not he has to dance with the others. In Transylvania the bride and two other girls hide behind a curtain, and the bridegroom has to guess which is the bride, while they all try to confuse him. Similar customs are found among several savage peoples. The bridesmaids of a modern wedding are probably a relic of the usage.[95] The only possible explanation of the custom seems to be the widespread belief in the primitive mind that supernatural dangers attend every marriage ; it is a great opportunity for evil spirits, and, in a later stage of culture, for witches. When there is a number of pretending brides, and the actual recognition comes at the last moment, the powers of evil are uncertain as to which is the real bride and are consequently baffled.

Leaving the more cheerful aspect of life, we find
that there are also children's games in use in England
to-day, as throughout the world, that imitate a
funeral. But it is curious that these games have
far fewer traces of anything primitive than the
marriage games. The game of *Jenny Jones*, which
exists in many versions, is a funeral game. The
name of the principal character has suffered many
corruptions ; in one Scottish version it has become
Genesis ! [96]—a tribute doubtless to the Biblical
knowledge of the Scottish child. It ought to be
Jenny jo—the old name for a sweetheart,[97] as in
' John Anderson, my jo John.'

The game begins with the chant :

> ' I come to see poor Jenny Jones,
>   Jenny Jones, Jenny Jones,
> I come to see poor Jenny Jones,
>   And how is she to-day ? '

The answer is :

> ' She's washing, she's washing,
>   And you can't see her to-day.'

and the visitors respond :

> ' Very well, ladies, ladies, ladies,
>   Very well, ladies, and gentlemen too.'

Then the first quatrain is repeated (as after every
answer) and the next reply is :

> ' She's folding, she's folding,
>   And you can't see her to-day.'

The game proceeds and the inquirers are next told :

> ' She's ironing, she's ironing,
>   And you can't see her to-day.'

Then a change comes over the spirit of the game, and the replies are, first that she is dying, and then that she is dead.

Then the visitors say :

> ' I come in my white dress, white dress, white dress,
> I come in my white dress, and how will that do ? '[98]

The answer is :

> ' White is for a wedding, a wedding, a wedding,
> White is for a wedding, and that won't do.'

Then the visitors propose various changes of costume, and are told successively :

> ' Blue is for sailors, for sailors, for sailors,
> Blue is for sailors, and that won't do.'

> ' Red is for soldiers, for soldiers, for soldiers,
> Red is for soldiers, and that won't do.'

Then the visitors say :

> ' I come in my black dress, black dress, black dress,
> I come in my black dress, and how will that do ? '

The reply is :

> ' Black is for a funeral,
> And that will do
> To carry poor Jenny to the grave.'[99]

Another funeral game is called *Booman*, and the formula is :

> ' Dill doule[100] for Booman,
> Booman is dead and gone,
> Left his wife all alone,
> And all his children.
> Where shall we bury him ?   Carry him to London ;
> By his grandfather's grave grows a green onion.
> Dig his grave wide and deep,
> Strew it with flowers,
> Toll the bell, toll the bell,
> Twenty-four hours ! '

The accompanying action is for the boys to carry the corpse to the grave, and lower it in, while the girls weep, and strew flowers on the way ; and for the boys to imitate the pulling of the bell-rope.[101]

Such games are also found in other lands. In France, for example, the game called *Le Roi de Maroc* is a funeral game. It is played with lighted candles (which, of course, are a part of the Catholic ritual at a funeral) and with the pretence of tears and sobs and beating of the breast. The words of the dialogue are :

> ' Ah ! quelle nouvelle ! '
> ' Hélas ! '
> ' Le roi de Maroc est mort ! '
> ' Hélas ! '
> ' Il est enterré ! '
> ' Hélas ! '
> ' Il s'est coupé le cou d'un coup de coutelas ! '
> ' Hélas ! hélas ! hélas ! et quatre fois hélas ! ' [102]

(" What news ? " "Alas ! " " The King of Morocco is dead ! " " Alas ! " " He is buried." " Alas ! " " He cut his throat from ear to ear ! " " Alas, alas, alas ! O dear ! " ')

There does not seem to be anything left of ancient usage in these funeral games except the custom, preserved in the game of *Booman,* of strewing flowers at the grave, which goes back to very early times. Thus at the Parentalia in ancient Rome, which was practically a yearly renewal of the rite of burial,[103] the family went in procession to the grave and strewed the place with flowers. So Virgil tells us Aeneas did at Anchises' tomb :

> Purpureosque iacit flores, ac talia fatur :
> Salve, sancte parens !

('With roses then the sepulchre he strowed,
And thus his father's ghost bespoke aloud,
Hail, holy sire ! ')[104]

The custom was general in our own land.   There
are many references to it in Shakespeare.   So in
Romeo and Juliet (IV, 5, 89) :

'Our bridal flowers serve for a buried corpse,'

and in the same play (V, 3, 281) :

'He came with flowers to strew his lady's grave.'

And in *The Winter's Tale* (IV, 4, 128–129), where
Perdita says :

'O, these I lack
To make you garlands of ; and my sweet friend,
To strew him o'er and o'er ! '

and Florizel replies :

'What, like a corse ?

And in *Cymbeline* (IV, 2, 218–222), where Guiderius
says :

'We have done our obsequies , come, lay him down,'

and Belarius goes on :

'Here's a few flowers, but 'bout midnight more
The herbs that have on them cold dew o' the night
Are strewings fitt'st for graves.'

CHAPTER III

SPRINGTIME AND VERDURE

THERE is a widespread custom among boys in England, on the 29th of May, of wearing an oak-leaf,[105] at least until noon ; anyone found without that talisman might be ' nettled ' by the other boys, who carried bunches of nettles in their pockets for the purpose.[106]   The accompanying rhyme was :

> ' Twenty-ninth of May,
>   Royal Oak Day ;
> If you don't give us holiday we'll all run away !

The latter words were supposed to be specially addressed to the schoolmaster. The custom was understood by everybody to refer to the Merry Monarch—the date to his birthday, and the oak-leaf to the tree which was his hiding-place after the battle of Worcester :

> ' —the famous oak
> Wherein the younger Charles abode,
>   Till all the paths were dim,
> And far below the Roundhead rode
>   And hummed a surly hymn.' [107]

There is, of course, historic warrant for this, to the extent that Charles II did hide in an oak, and that the 29th of May, as his birthday, and also the date of his triumphant entry into London, was established as a public holiday. It was in September 1651 that Charles hid himself in the oak at Boscobel, and it was nearly nine years later that the 29th of May was proclaimed as a day of national rejoicing. On the 1st of June 1660 Pepys recorded in his *Diary* that ' at night Mr. Cooke comes from London with letters, leaving all things there very gallant and joyful ; and brought us word that the Parliament had ordered the 29th of May, the King's birthday, to be for ever kept as a day of thanksgiving for our redemption from tyranny, and the King's return to his government, he entering London that day.'

But the wearing of the oak-leaf is undoubtedly a relic of some prehistoric festival of spring, marked by the display of green foliage, and this detail has become connected, in comparatively recent times, with a historic name and a historic event ; for games and customs which possess the essential characteristic are found in lands which never owed loyalty to the Stuarts, and in ages long before the dynasty existed. In some parts of the United States to-day a game is played which consists of challenging a child with the word ' Green ! ' The child so accosted must produce something green, such as a leaf of a tree, or a blade of grass, or else pay a forfeit. The children rarely go abroad, it is said, without some piece of verdure hidden in the pocket, or in the shoe, or somewhere about the person, and the practice almost amounts to a superstition.[108] But this very game is mentioned long ago by Rabelais as one of those played by Gargantua,[109] and it is still played in France with the formula, ' *Je vous prends sans vert !* '—' I catch you without green ! '

It is stated that at Châtillon-sur-Inde it is played during Lent, and only after the Angelus.[110]   In the Middle Ages it seems to have been played in the month of May, with the same formula, and a drenching with water as the penalty.[111]   In the seventeenth century it was a fashionable game amongst aristocratic folk in Paris.   The plot of a comedy attributed to La Fontaine is based upon the usage.   In the eighteenth century there were actually *Sans vert* clubs at Metz which adopted some particular herb or leaf as a badge ; any member challenged had to produce it, and if he failed to do so he had to pay a fine, which went to provide funds for a dinner or a dance.[112]

In all these cases the practice of wearing green leaves is plainly the survival of a prehistoric rite which once had a solemn significance.   It would fill a volume if we were even to summarize all the evidence that has been collected as to the existence throughout the world of festivals of spring.   These were generally celebrated at the beginning of May in Europe,[113] or at some date corresponding to that season in other latitudes, and they were nearly always associated with the decoration of houses, or persons, or some special structure erected for the occasion, with the green foliage which had then begun to appear.   There is no doubt at all that these festivals were originally magical rites connected with the renewal of vegetation.   All this is very natural ; the passing of the winter was the passing of darkness and death ; the coming of the spring was the advent of light and life, and it must have made a profound impression upon the mind of early man.

There are classical survivals of such festivals of spring. The festival of the Floralia at Rome, for example, was held on the last days of April and the first days of May. There is considerable obscurity as to this festival, but it is at least clear that it was connected with fertility. The tradition was that the games had been introduced in consequence of a dearth, which was also the alleged reason for the institution of the Cerialia ; there was probably a close relation between Ceres and Flora. The vetches, beans, and lupines which were scattered among the people in the Circus Maximus on the occasion of the festival also point to a rite of fertility.[114]

There are examples of such festivals of spring, gathering around the conception of fructification, in many lands. Sometimes the festival has retained very plain traces of the human sacrifice that formerly was part of it. Very often the chief actor in it is disguised in green foliage, and there is a pretence of putting him to death. The leafy framework in which all such personages are encased reminds us at once of the great figures constructed of osiers or covered with grass in which the Druids enclosed and burned their human victims.[115] Thus in Saxony at Whitsuntide the rite is ' Fetching the Wild Man out of the Wood '. The performer is clothed in leaves and moss, and hides in the forest. The lads of the village go out to find him, and take him captive. They fire at him with blank charges and he pretends to fall down dead. A boy who personates a physician then bleeds him and he comes to life again, whereupon they bind him on a wagon, take him to the village, and tell everybody that they

have caught ' The Wild Man '.[116] So at Nieder-
pöring in Lower Bavaria the *Pfingstl* was a boy clad
from head to foot in leaves and flowers. He was
taken round the village by two boys, with drawn
swords, who expected to receive gifts at every
house where they called. The people hid, and
drenched the leafy boy with water. Finally he
waded into a brook, and one of his attendants,
standing on the bridge, pretended to cut off his
head.[117] On Whit Monday in Bohemia a man
known as ' The King ' is dressed in a robe of bark
adorned with flowers. He is led captive around the
village, chased out of every house where the party
calls, and finally there is the pretence of beheading
him.[118] In some parts of Russia on St. George's
Day a youth is dressed out in leaves and flowers.
The Slovenes call him ' Green George '. He goes
in procession through the cornfields. There is a
similar custom, with a similar name, in Carinthia,
Transylvania, and Roumania.[119]

Now all these are undoubtedly representations of
the spirit of vegetation manifesting itself in the new
life and the green foliage of spring. The element of
sacrifice points back to the time when a human
victim was offered to promote the growth of the
crops ; the sacrifice seems to have typified the dead
vegetation of winter, and the victim has sometimes
been generalized, apparently, into ' Winter ' or
' Death ', and has also become a kind of general
scapegoat. So we find that there has been in many
places about this time of the year a custom of
' carrying out Death '. In Bohemia during Lent
the young people throw into the water a puppet
called Death, and then the girls go into the wood,

cut down a young tree, fasten to it a puppet dressed in white, and go round the village singing songs with the refrain :

> ' We carry Death out of the village
> We bring Summer into the village.'[120]

So in Bavaria during Lent the boys used to make a straw effigy of Death, which was carried through the streets with burlesque state, and then burned beyond the bounds.[121] So in many other places, as in some villages of Thuringia, where the carrying out of the puppet was accompanied by a song beginning : ' Now we carry Death out of the village and Spring into the village ! ' Olaus Magnus tells us that there was a similar custom in Sweden, in the sixteenth century. On the first day of May the young men formed two troops for a mimic fight— one party headed by a man clothed in skins who threw about snowballs and pieces of ice, the other headed by a man clothed in green leaves and boughs. It was called ' driving away Winter and receiving Summer '.[122]

Many of these rites have left considerable traces in popular customs as well as in children's games. The most striking of these in our own land are probably the May-pole and Jack-in-the-Green. The May-pole still exists in some English villages, and our older literature is full of references to it. In a village it would often be the most outstanding object : it is an English proverb, ' As tall as a May-pole '. Even among the higher buildings of a city it was sometimes conspicuous : [123] the Church of St. Andrew-Undershaft in the city of London

derives its name from the fact that it was under
the towering ' shaft ' of the May-pole in Cornhill,
' which shaft ', says Stow, ' when it was set on end
and fixed in the ground, was higher than the church
steeple '.[124] Stow goes on to tell how a preacher
at Paul's Cross said that this May-pole was an idol,
and how the people took it down from the hooks
where it hung under the eaves of a row of houses in
Shaft Alley, sawed it up, and burned it.

Later on May-poles became more and more a
matter of contention between the Puritans and their
opponents. The setting up of May-poles on Sundays
had been expressly allowed and encouraged by the
warrant of Charles I,[125] dated the 18th of October
1633, which was a republication of the *Declaration
of Sports* that had been issued by his father. Eleven
years later the Parliament suppressed them altogether. The ordinance, dated the 6th of April 1644
said : ' And because the prophanation of the Lord's
Day hath been heretofore greatly occasioned by
May-poles (a heathenish vanity, generally abused
to superstition and wickednesse), the Lords and
Commons do further order and ordain, that all and
singular May-poles, that are or shall be erected,
shall be taken down and removed by the constables,
borsholders, tything men, petty constables and
churchwardens of the parishes, when the same be ;
and that no May-pole shall be hereafter set up,
erected, or suffered to be within this kingdom of
England or dominion of Wales '.[126]

A Puritan writer in the time of Elizabeth has
described the bringing home of the May-pole from
the woods, with ' twentie or fourtie yoke of Oxen,
euery Oxe havyng a sweete Nosegaie of flowers tyed

on the tippe of his hornes, and these Oxen drawe
home this Maie-poole (this stinckyng Idoll rather)
which is couered all ouer with Flowers and Hearbes,
bounde rounde aboute with stringes, from the top
to the bottome '.[127] This description is noteworthy
in its details, especially as to the ' flowers and
hearbes ' with which the May-pole was decorated ;
for it is significant that when the May-pole is merely
a bare pole, and a permanent fixture, it is still
decorated with foliage and flowers at the festival.
Originally it was a living tree brought out of the
forest every year for the occasion. So it has been
in recent times and perhaps is still in various parts
of Europe.

The May-pole, May-bush, or Green Man, as
representing a spirit of fertility, can cause abundance
in other things besides the fruits of the earth.
Consequently we find bushes and branches of trees
used as a charm for milch cows. Down to a time
within living memory farmers in Scotland used to
put up boughs of mountain ash in the cow-byres on
the second day of May.[128] The Irish used to fasten
a green bough of a tree on the house on May Day,
and believed that it would bring an abundance of
milk that summer. A custom of setting up May-
bushes at the doors of the byres with a similar
intention existed in Germany.[129] So at the Parilia
in ancient Rome, in the month of April, the sheep-
folds were decked with green boughs, and a garland
was hung on the gate.[130]

Generally the May-bush or the May-garland was
regarded as bringing good luck. In various parts
of England a tree or a bush was placed before every
house on May Day, with flowers strewn around it.[131]

Spenser describes the custom in *The Shepheard's Calender* :

> ' Yougthes folke now flocken in everywhere,
> To gather May buskets and smelling brere :
> And home they hasten the postes to dight
> And all the Kirke pillours eare daylight,
> With hawthorn buds and swete eglantine,
> And girlonds of roses, and sopps in wine.'[132]

Similarly, Herrick bids Corinna, when they are going a-Maying :

> ' marke
> How each field turns a street, each street a parke
> Made green, and trimmed with trees ; see how
> Devotion gives each house a bough
> Or branch ; each porch, each doore, ere this,
> An arke, a tabernacle is,
> Made up of white thorn[133] neatly interwove.'

So there was a general custom in most regions of England for the young people to rise a little after midnight on the morning of the first of May, and go into the woods,[134] where they broke off branches and then decked them with flowers. A sixteenth-century writer tells us that people go from every parish ' against Maie, to the woods and the groves, some to the hilles and mountaines, some to one place, some to another, where they spende all the night in pastymes, and in the mornyng they returne, bringing with them birch, bowes, and braunches of trees to deck their assemblies withall '.[135]

Frequently this custom was associated with memories of Robin Hood, and some of those who took part in it were dressed up to represent the bold outlaw and his associates. Probably the association of Robin Hood and his merry men with the greenwood is enough to account for this. So it is recorded

that on May Day of the year 1516 King Henry VIII
and Queen Katherine ' rode a-maying from Green-
wich to the high ground of Shooters Hill, where as
they passed by the way they espied a companie of
tall yeomen, cloathed all in greene, with greene
hoodes, and with bowes and arrows, to the number
of two hundred. One, being their chieftaine, was
called Robin Hoode, who desired the King and
Queene with their retinue to enter the greene wood,
where in harbours made of boughs and decked with
flowers, they were set and served plentifully with
venison and wine by Robin Hoode and his
meynie '.[136]

The game *Here we Come Gathering Nuts and May*
(it ought to be ' Knots of May ') appears to have
been a May-game of this sort originally, though it
has become approximated in practice to games of
capture. It used to be played in Derbyshire with
branches of May-blossom waved over the heads of
the players.[137] In some places young people went
about on May morning singing :

> ' We've been rambling all the night
> And sometime of this day ;
> And now returning back again,
> We bring a garland gay.

> A garland gay we bring you here ;
> And at your door we stand ;
> It is a sprout well budded out,
> The work of our Lord's hand.'[138]

So the εἰρεσιώνη in ancient Greece was a bough
or a wreath borne around by singing boys at the
festivals of the Thargelia and the Pyanopsia and
afterward hung up at the door of the house.[139]

The custom of going about on May Day with

garlands was kept up particularly by the milkmaids of London. They wore wreaths of flowers on their heads and also decked their milk-pails with garlands. Pepys has a reference to the custom, and to Nell Gwynne watching it. On the 1st of May 1667 he records that he went ' to Westminster, meeting many milkmaids with their garlands upon their pails, dancing with a fiddler before them, and saw pretty Nelly standing at her lodgings' door in Drury Lane in her smock sleeves and bodice, looking upon one : she seemed a mighty pretty creature '.

A hundred years ago women sold May-garlands in the streets of Newcastle-on-Tyne on May morning with the song :

> ' Rise up, maidens, fie for shame !
> For I've been four long miles from hame,
> I've been gathering my garlands gay ;
> Rise up, fair maids, and take in your May.'[140]

One of the most striking examples of survival in this connexion is the personage known as Jack-in-the-Green, usually a chimney-sweep who walks about encased in a framework of foliage, which is generally holly and ivy.[141] This was kept up in London as late as 1818,[142] and it still survives in some places, as, for example, at Knutsford in Cheshire, though the connexion with chimney-sweeps seems generally to have ceased, and in some cases the festival has been transferred to the 29th of the month. Thus at Castleton in Derbyshire, on Royal Oak Day, ' a great garland of wild flowers is made, shaped like a bell on a frame, and it is carried round the town by a man on horseback, who wears it upon his head covering his face. He plays

Charles II, the part of the Queen who rides beside him is taken by a youth dressed in a lady's riding habit and veil. Twenty girls dance the Morris dance before them as they ride through the town '.[143]

Another curious survival, probably belonging to the same range of ideas, was the Jack-o'-Lent. This was a puppet that was pelted with missiles, as in the other cruel custom of pelting cocks at Shrovetide.[144] There are a good many references to the Jack-o'-Lent in Elizabethan literature. Thus Falstaff, after he has 'begun to perceive that he is made an ass', says : 'See now how wit may be made a Jack-a-Lent, when 'tis upon ill employment !' [145] and Quarles writes in his *Shepheard's Oracles* :

'How like a Jack o' Lent
He stands, for boys to spend their Shrovetide throws,
Or like a puppet made to frighten crows.'

There are not many references, apparently, to the survival of the custom in later days. Almost the only one we have found relates to the little town of Polperro, in Cornwall, some seventy or eighty years ago. 'An old custom, now quite defunct, was observed here not long since in the beginning of Lent. A figure made up of straw and cast-off clothes was carried round the town, amid much noise and merriment, after which it was either burnt, shot at, or brought to some other ignominious end. This image was called " Jack-o'-Lent ". . . . A dirty slovenly fellow is often termed a Jack o' Lent.' [146] Another usage in which a puppet was employed (but not abused in this instance) was the children's custom of carrying about dolls, decked with flowers and lying in little boxes, on the 29th of

May. They were called 'May-babies'.[147] This obtained in many parts of England until quite recently.

There are other children's games which are obviously related to ritual dances, often held in the spring. The motive is rather more special than in the general festivals of spring, for the original intention here is to encourage the growth of particular crops, and often crops where length of fibre is specially wanted. The significance of some of these games is scarcely obvious at first sight. There is, for example, a familiar game played with the formula :

> ' How many miles to Babylon ? '
> ' Three score and ten.'
> ' Can we get there by candle-light ? '
> ' Yes, and back again ! '

In some versions ' Babylon ' is replaced by ' Hebron ', or ' Bethlehem ', or ' London ', or ' Banbury ', or ' Burslem ', or ' Barley-bridge '.[148] The essential action is for two of the players to join their hands and lift up their arms, making an arch, while the rest of the players pass through. In one variety of the game the players, as they pass through, are divided into two groups, and there is finally a tug of war between them.

There does not appear to be anything very significant in this. But the game is connected with another extremely interesting game, for one rhyme goes :

> ' How many miles to Hebron ? '
> ' Three score and ten.'
> ' Shall I be there by midnight ? '
> ' Yes, and back again.'
> ' Then, *thread the needle* ! '[149]

Now there is an English game, *Thread the Needle,*
which is played much in the same way as *How Many
Miles to Babylon ?* but with the formula :

> ' Thread the needle through the skin,
> Sometimes out and sometimes in.'

When the lines of players get entangled, they jog
up and down, and say :

> ' A bundle o' rags, a bundle o' rags.'

And there is a game called *Threading the Needle,*
recorded in Massachusetts, with the formula :

> ' The needle's eye
> That doth supply
> The thread that runs so true ;
> Ah ! many a lass
> Have I let pass
> Because I wanted you ! '[150]

The action is for a boy and a girl to make an
arch of their hands, under which the other players
pass, until the hands drop, and one of the players is
caught.   A game called *Thread the Needle* used to
be played at Trowbridge and Bradford-on-Avon on
Shrove Tuesday, and at Evesham on Easter
Monday.[151]   At Baldock in Hertfordshire the revels
on May Day always ended with *Thread the Needle*
(otherwise called *Needle Tick*), which was danced
up and down and all around the place by great
numbers of children.   This was kept at least as late
as the end of the eighteenth century.[152]

The game is apparently derived from a ritual
dance, and every student of the past knows the
magical and religious significance of dancing.
Lucian declared that there was not a single ancient
mystery in which there was not dancing, and that

'to dance out the mysteries' (ἐξορχεῖσθαι τὰ
μυστήρια) was a common phrase used of completing
the ritual.[153]   Very often the dance had a reference
to the coming of spring, and the growth of the
crops.   Thus in Greece the dance of the Kouroi, or
initiate youths, in the dithyramb, was a magic
dance to celebrate, or rather to help forward, the
advent of spring and the growth of vegetation.[154]
So in Rome the Salii, or dancing priests, went
through the city in March and in October—the
Romans sowed their seed in spring and autumn—
dancing, leaping, singing, and clashing their spears
against their shields.   They were priests of Mars,
and Mars was not only the god of war, but of
agriculture ;   there cannot be much doubt that
there was an agricultural significance about the rite
originally.[155]

One could fill hundreds of pages with examples,
drawn from all over the world, of rites of dancing
and leaping which are manifestly connected with
agriculture.   Some relics of these ritual dances
survive to-day.   One is still kept up at Helston in
Cornwall.   It is called the *Furry Dance*, and is
celebrated on the 8th of May.[156]   Another name for
it is the *Faddy* (apparently from *fade*, a Cornish word
meaning 'to go').[157]   A song used to be sung on
the occasion, 'the whole of which' (an eighteenth
century correspondent of the *Gentleman's Magazine*
writes)[158] 'nobody now recollects, and of which I
know no more than that there is mention in it of
"the grey goose quill", and of going "to the green
wood to bring home the Summer and the May
O".' [159]   Flowering branches of hawthorn used to
be worn in the headgear.   About midday the folk

4

gathered together, and danced around the town to a
traditional tune, claiming the right to pass through
any of the houses. The dance went on until dark.[160]
Though it still survives it seems to have lost some
of its earlier features.

There was another curious dance at St. Roche,
and one or two other adjacent parishes, in the
second week of June, at the time of the annual
' feast '. It was called *The Snail's Creep*. The
leaders of the dance moved in a narrowing circle,
and the followers became coiled around in concentric
circles. When all the performers were massed
together the leaders began to retrace the spiral.[161]
The dance was directed by young men who waved
leafy branches.

Some of these dances retained plain traces of an
earlier ritual of sacrifice. There was a dance at
Kirtlington, for example, where a maiden was chosen
as the central figure. It was regarded as vital that
she should be of blameless character ; she was
dressed in white ; and she was invested for the day
with a sort of sanctity, so that anyone was fined if
he even jostled her in the crowd. Later on a lamb
was substituted for the girl, and was taken round
the village as the centre of the dance.[162] At
Kidlington also there was a dance on the Monday
after Whitsuntide, and there a lamb was pursued
by the girls. The one who caught the lamb with
her teeth was proclaimed *The Lady of the Lamb*.
The lamb was killed, and carried about on a pole to
the village green, where there was a dance around
it. The next day the lamb was cooked and eaten
at a solemn feast.[163]

A ritual dance has been kept up in times past in

England by young people of both sexes on particular
days in the year, generally about the month of May,
in which, in some cases, they finally attempted to
encircle the parish church with joined hands. This
custom of encircling the church with linked hands
(though apparently without a dance) was kept up
at Birmingham into the late years of the eighteenth
century. On Easter Monday the charity children thus surrounded the two churches which the
town then possessed. It was called ' clipping the
churches '.[164] The custom was also kept up by
children in Wiltshire on Shrove Tuesday with the
accompanying rhyme :

' Shrove Tuesday, Shrove Tuesday, Jack went to plough,
His mother made pancakes, she scarcely knew how,
She tossed them, she turned them, she made them so black
With soot from the chimney that poisoned poor Jack.'[165]

In some cases the dancers imitated the actions either
of husbandry or of weaving. So Giraldus Cam-
brensis tells us that at the Church of St. Almedda,
near Brecknock, there was in his day a solemn
festival in honour of the saint, held at the beginning
of August, when the people danced around the
churchyard, sometimes falling to the ground as in
a trance, sometimes springing up as in a frenzy ;
and representing with their hands and feet different
kinds of work, one man pretending to guide the
plough, another to goad the oxen. ' Now you may
see a girl with the distaff, drawing out the thread,
and winding it again on the spindle ; another
walking, and arranging the threads for the web ;
another, as it were, throwing the shuttle, and
seeming to weave.' [166]

Now, there is a children's game recorded both in England and in America, called *Oats and Beans and Barley Grow*. The English formula is :

> ' Oats and beans and barley grow !
> Do you or I or anyone know
> How oats and beans and barley grow ?
> First the farmer sows his seed
> Then he stands and takes his ease
> Thumps his foot and claps his hand,
> And turns him round to view the land.'

Then the game merges into the usual choosing a partner. The action of sowing the seed is imitated when the relevant words are spoken.[167]

There are close parallels to this in many lands in Europe, from Sweden to Sicily. Thus the very interesting French game called *L'Avoine* [168] imitates by appropriate action the farmer sowing the oats and resting a little, leaping in the air, and then mowing, binding, and threshing the oats. The accompanying words are :

> ' Qui veut ouïr, qui veut scavoir
> Comme on sème l'avoine ?
> Mon père la semoit ainsi.'

The player pretends to sow the seed

> ' Puis se reposoit un petit.
> Tapoit des pieds,
> Battoit des mains,
> Et faisoit le tour du vilain,
> Avoine, avoine, avoine,
> Le beau temps te ramène.'

Here the children take hands, and leap up together.

> (' Would you hear, and would you know
> How their oats the farmers sow ?

Thus my father sows the seed,
Then he rests a little while ;
Stamps his foot,
Claps his hand,
And turns about to see the land ;
Oats, oats, oats, we sow,
And the fine weather makes them grow.')

Then :

    ' Qui veut ouïr, qui veut sçavoir
    Comment on fauche l'avoine ?
    Mone père la fauchoit ainsi.'

Here the player pretends to mow the corn.

    ' Puis se reposit un petit
    Tapoit des pieds, battoit des mains,
    Et faisoit le tour du vilain.
    Avoine, avoine, avoine,
    Le beau temps te ramène.'

And so on with the action of binding, threshing, and winnowing the oats. There are references to the game in Froissart and Rabelais.

Now the most interesting detail here is the action of leaping, after the oats are sown. For it is eloquent of what underlies all these games and dances—the universal belief of primitive man in what is called sympathetic magic. All things in the world are connected by similarities, and consequently things in external nature and things in human life mutually react upon each other. Thus a process of growth or of decay anywhere may affect the increase or decrease of something else. You should therefore always sow your seed in a waxing moon, because as the moon increases in apparent size the seed will grow.[169] On the other hand, in the neighbourhood of the sea, anyone who is near death will die as the tide goes out, for the

soul will pass out as the water ebbs.[170]   So Mistress
Quickly told of Falstaff's death, that ' a' parted
even just between twelve and one, even at the
turning o' the tide '.[171] Not only do natural
processes affect human affairs, but human actions
may similarly affect natural processes. So that to
leap high in the air is to encourage the hemp to
grow tall, and to wind about in the long line of a
dance is to enable the flax to grow long. At La
Châtre hundreds of French peasants used to perform
a dance which was called by the very same name
as the children's game we have mentioned, *Threading
the Needle*, and when they were asked the why and
the wherefore of it, they answered, ' To make the
hemp grow ! ' [172]   So in Herefordshire fires of straw
were made on Twelfth Day, as late as 1822 at least.
The largest was ' to burn the old witch '.   The
country folk sang and danced around the fires, and
it is significant to read that ' without this festival
they think that they should have no crop.' [173]   So
in Franche-Comté they say that you should dance
at the Carnival in order to make the hemp grow tall.
In Swabia and several other parts of Germany it is
a common custom for a man who has sown hemp to
leap high on the field, in the belief that this will
make the hemp grow high.   In the Vosges the man
who sows hemp pulls up his breeches as far as he
can, and it is thought that the hemp will reach the
height to which he succeeds in perilously hitching
them up.[174]   In Baden there was a dance called
the ' Hemp Dance ' on Shrove Tuesday, and so in
other parts of Germany and Austria.   In some parts
of eastern Prussia the girls dance one by one in a
large hoop at midnight on Shrove Tuesday.   The

hoop is adorned with leaves, flowers, and ribbons, and attached to it are a small bell and some flax. While dancing within the hoop each girl has to wave her arms vigorously and cry ' Flax grow ! ' or words to that effect. In Anhalt when the sower had sowed the flax he leaped up and flung the seed-bag high in the air, saying, ' Grow and turn green ! You have nothing else to do '.[175] It may be significant that skipping, as a girl's game, prevails during the spring months of the year—the months when the seed is springing up. Both skipping and swinging probably connect with the dancing and leaping that have been described as a ritual relating to the growth of the crops. It looks unnecessary to seek a recondite origin for anything as simple as a child's swing. The child delights in the swaying motion, and that is enough, one would think, to account for the device. But there is a good deal of curious evidence that the exercise of swinging was seriously practised as a magical rite. Thus in Siam a substitute monarch popularly known as ' King Hop ', because during some ceremonies he has to stand on one leg (his proper title is ' Lord of the Heavenly Host ') is taken in procession to an open space facing the temple of the Brahmans, where there are a number of poles dressed like May-poles. In his presence the Brahmans swing through the air, at a height of ninety feet, on a swing suspended between two of these poles. Meanwhile King Hop must keep his right foot from the ground. This latter detail is thought by the Siamese to be connected with the stability of the throne and State. But the other activities of King Hop in the spring evidently relate to the fertility of the ground and the abundance of the crops,[176] and it is pretty certain that the swinging has some such reference. So in the Celebes young girls used to swing at ceremonies connected with the harvest. So did young people of both sexes in Nepal at the great festival before the cutting of the rice ; sometimes they swung from a framework of bamboos, sometimes from the boughs of trees. (There is a notorious and ghastly rite in India of men swinging on hooks thrust through the flesh of their shoulders.) Among the Dyaks of Sarawak the men swing, sometimes a dozen together, chanting an invocation to the spirits for a good harvest. At some festivals in Dardistan the women swing on ropes suspended from trees. In Borneo priests receive communications from the spirits as they rock to and fro on swings. There was a swinging festival at Athens, and a myth about the death of Icarius and his daughter Erigone was related to account for it. The women in various parts of Greece still swing ceremonially about the time of Easter. In Calabria, where there was much early Greek influence, the girls now swing solemnly on Christmas Day.[177]   It is said that between Easter and St. John's Day the Lettish peasants spend their leisure in swinging, because the higher you rise in the air as you swing, the higher the flax will grow that season. In ancient Rome swinging seems to have formed a ritual part of the great Latin festival, and there was a very interesting custom then (as at other festivals) of hanging up balls, masks, and small images of the human figure, on trees or in doorways, to swing in the wind. The name of these figures was *oscilla*, and the fact that they swung in the wind suggested a verb *oscillare*, which has passed into English as *oscillate*.[178] The *oscilla* were evidently imitations of men and women, and probably substitutes for them. Virgil describes the custom of the farmers :

> Et te, Bacche, vocant per carmina laeta, tibique
> Oscilla ex alta suspendunt mollia pinu.[179]
>
> (' They hail thee, Bacchus, in their merry lines,
> And hang the swinging puppets on the pines.')

There is much evidence, of course, to show that puppets were often substituted for human beings in sacrifices, and in other rites.

The precise significance of this custom of swinging is somewhat obscure. Sometimes it seems to have reference to the winter solstice, as if it were an attempt to help the sun to swing higher in the sky. Sometimes it seems to be intended as a purification of the air, and one is reminded of the curious remark of Athanasius that Christ died in the air that He might purify the air, which is the special domain of the Devil and of demons. ' This must be done through death, and by what other kind of death could this be done except a death in the air, I mean, on the Cross ? For he alone dies in the air who finishes his life upon a cross.' [180] Sometimes, and most often, it has reference to the crops, and is evidently a suggestion to the seed that it shall grow high, and sway in the wind. As we have seen, there is a custom widely distributed in the world (and found until quite recently in Germany) by which those who are sowing seed leap as high as they can at every few steps, that the hemp or the flax may grow as high as they leap. This belongs to the same range of ideas.

When our children nowadays skip and swing as a game they are in the line of descent from a very ancient magical custom. It is curious that some versions of a swinging rhyme preserve a reference to fairies, who may be presumed here to have succeeded the spirits of the air :

> ' See-saw, Margery Daw,
> Sold her bed and lay upon straw ;
> She sold her straw and lay upon hay,
> *Piskies came and carried her away !* '[181]

CHAPTER IV

SUNSHINE AND FIRE

ON the night of the 5th of November all
England is ablaze. For weeks before the
boys collect money for fireworks and fuel for
bonfires. Every one is familiar with the weird
effigy which they carry about on the day, and with
the rhyme which they recite as they go their rounds :

> ' Please to remember
> The fifth of November,
> Gunpowder treason and plot.
> I see no reason
> Why Gunpowder treason
> Should ever be forgot ! '[182]

In Scotland the rhyme was :

> ' The Gunpowder Plot
> Will never be forgot
> While Edinburgh Castle stands on a rock.'[183]

The mention of the Castle is perhaps connected
with the fact that the Castle guns used to be fired
on the 5th of November.[184]

This engaging ritual, as everybody knows, is in
memory of the famous seventeenth-century plot,
the most picturesque conspirator in which was Guy
Fawkes. Some of the rhymes recited on the day
remember his name :

> ' Guy Fawkes and his companions did the plot contrive
> To blow the King and Parliament all up alive ;
> But, by God's providence, him they catch,
> With a dark lantern, lighting a match ! '[185]

The plot was engineered by some of the more reckless Catholics. They had hoped for relief under James I, but his first Parliament, which met in 1604, was Puritan in feeling, and pressed for increased severity in the laws against Catholics. Accordingly a number of conspirators, of whom the chief were Robert Catesby, Thomas Winter, and Guy Fawkes, devised a bold and callous plot. They managed to hire some cellars under the House of Lords, and stored barrels of gunpowder there, with the purpose of blowing up the whole assembly when Parliament met. A disguised warning of the peril was conveyed to several Catholic peers, and it was through this that the conspirators' plans became known to the Government. The meeting of Parliament, after several postponements, was finally fixed for the 5th of November 1605. The cellars were searched at the last moment and Fawkes was discovered ready to fire the train.

Guy Fawkes was a native of York—the entry of his baptism is still shown to visitors in the register of the Church of St. Michael-le-Belfrey, beneath the shadow of the minster. His father died when Guy was nine years of age. Some years afterwards his mother married again, her second husband being a Catholic. It must have been while Guy lived in his stepfather's house at Scotton that he became a fanatical Catholic, for his own father and his mother hitherto had been Protestants. Shortly after coming of age the young man disposed of his estate (for he was quite well-to-do) and enlisted in the Spanish army. He was present at the capture of Calais by the Spaniards in 1595. After the death of Queen Elizabeth, Fawkes was employed

for a time in some diplomatic work on behalf of the
Catholics.

He does not seem to have had any original part
in devising the Gunpowder Plot. That was the
work of Robert Catesby and Thomas Winter. But
Fawkes was known to these men—he had accompanied Catesby to Bergen in 1604, to interview
Velasco, the Spanish envoy, on his way to the English
Court. When all hope of relief for the Catholics by
way of diplomatic intervention from Spain had been
given up, Catesby swore Fawkes to secrecy, and then
initiated him into the plot, along with Thomas
Percy. They approved of the scheme, and the
agreement was solemnly sealed by a Mass celebrated
by Gerard the Jesuit.

When Fawkes was arrested, Catesby had almost
immediate word of it, and accompanied by John
Wright fled into the midlands. Christopher Wright,
Thomas Percy, Ambrose Rookwood, and Thomas
Winter followed within a few hours. On the evening
of the 7th of November the party of conspirators,
by this time more than thirty in number, reached
Stephen Littleton's house at Holbeche, near Stour-
bridge, on the borders of Staffordshire. The next
morning, when they were preparing for the defence
of the house, and drying a store of gunpowder which
had been wetted, it exploded, by a very appropriate
accident, and several of them were hurt. A few
hours afterwards Sir Richard Walsh arrived with
his force, and besieged them. Catesby, Percy, and
John Wright were killed. The rest of the conspirators were captured, and in due course tried and
executed.

The Parliament which Guy Fawkes had meant to

blow up met on the appointed date, the 5th of November 1605. Four days later it was prorogued by the King, in order that there might be time for further inquiry into the plot. When it met again in January 1606 an Act was passed ordaining that the 5th of November should be kept as a day of national thanksgiving for ever. The Act was in force for more than two hundred and fifty years.[186]

How is it that the day has continued to be a popular festival for youth down to the present time, when all the passionate feeling about the Gunpowder Plot has long since passed away ? There cannot be the smallest doubt that, as in the case of Royal Oak Day, the celebration persists because a historic memory has become grafted on to a prehistoric rite.

For there was a widespread practice in early times of kindling bonfires at particular seasons of the year as a magic ritual. In spring the most frequent days were the first Sunday in Lent, Easter Eve, and the first day of May. In summer, the fires were always on Midsummer Day or Midsummer Eve. In winter they were on Christmas Day or Twelfth Night, in some cases, and in many others, on Hallowe'en,[187] the last day of October. It is perhaps significant that this last date is so near to the 5th of November—the fires associated with Hallowe'en probably merged into those associated with Guy Fawkes. The fact that the occasions of these ritual fires are dated according to the calendar of the Church is largely accidental, of course. In each case an old heathen ritual has perpetuated itself into Christian times, and the dates on which the rite was originally observed, with a primitive reference to the beginning of spring or the beginning of winter, or to the middle and end of the year, have been noted by, and in some cases perhaps approximated to, the date of a Christian festival, such as Easter or Christmas.

It is noticeable that two of these dates, May Eve (called *Walpurgis-Nacht* in Germany) and Hallowe'en, were two of the four principal witch-festivals, the others being Candlemas (the 2nd of February) and Lammas (the 1st of August), otherwise called the Gule of August.[188] There is not the slightest doubt, in view of modern researches, that the practice of mediaeval witchcraft was in fact the survival of primitive nature cults, so that it is not wonderful that some of these dates coincided, for the witch-festival and the fire-festival alike belonged to the same range of prehistoric religious usage.

The most important season for these fire-festivals in Europe has been the summer solstice, that is, Midsummer Day or Midsummer Eve. Midsummer Day, in the calendar of the Church, was the feast of St. John the Baptist, and hence the fires were often called St. John's fires. The rite has prevailed over the whole of Europe, and it is found in other places also. In Peru, where the sun was worshipped, the principal festivals were at the solstices and the equinoxes, and at Midsummer great fires were kindled, always by the sun's rays or by friction of wood, all household fires being previously extinguished. The great features of the rite in Europe in historic times were the bonfires, the rolling of a fiery wheel down a hill, and often a procession with torches around the fields.[189] The custom appears to survive to the present day in various parts of Europe, for example, in Bavaria, Bohemia, and

Brittany. In our own islands the Midsummer fires
were kept up, at any rate until the later years of
the eighteenth century, in various parts of England,
particularly Cornwall, Gloucestershire, and the
northern counties.[190] In some places they survived
to a still later period. It is stated that bonfires
were kindled in the streets of Sunderland on midsummer night until well within living memory, and
that it was the custom of the spectators to leap
through the flames.[191] There were bale-fires in
Ireland (and among the Irish community at Liver-
pool) on St. John's Eve, at least as late as 1867.[192]

The midsummer rite was the greatest of all these
fire-festivals, and with its accompaniments of dances
and sacrifices (very often, in the earlier periods,
human sacrifices) it was certainly the chief ceremony
of the year among the races of Europe. It was a
magic rite intended to increase the power of the
sun and—what was so clearly dependent upon that
—the fruitfulness of the earth. Then there became
connected with this latter, by a natural transition,
the thought of the fecundity of cattle, and of men
and women.[193] And then there seems to have been
superimposed upon this a general notion of purging
away the sins of the people. It is not so easy to
trace the connexion of the last with what has gone
before ; probably the notion of a renewal of light
and life began to suggest that the transgressions of
the unrenewed past ought to be both abjured and
expiated.

The first intention of the festival fires, however,
was to renew the fire of the sun, and though the
dates at which the fires were kindled ranged through
three of the four seasons of the year, the same

motive may be discerned on all the different occasions. In spring the sun was growing in strength, but was in need of encouragement, for still more sunshine was needed for the fruits of the earth. In midsummer the sun had reached its greatest strength, but it would henceforth decline. In winter the sun was at its weakest, and therefore all the more obviously needed reinforcement. The thought in the mind of primitive man is excellently illustrated by what Plutarch tells us of the Egyptians. He states that ' on the eighth day from the end of the month Phaophi they celebrate the festival of The Sun's Walking Stick, after the autumnal equinox, signifying that he requires as it were a support, and strengthening, as he grows weak both in heat and in light, and moves away from us, bending down, and crooked.' [194] Plutarch does not tell us whether this festival was celebrated with fires, but in most cases fire was the essential part of the ritual. The fire was meant to reinforce the sun's fire, in accordance with those notions of sympathetic magic that prevailed so largely in the primitive mind, and do still prevail so largely in the savage mind. Thus in New Caledonia when a wizard wants to make sunshine he climbs a mountain at daybreak, and sets fire to a bundle of charms at the moment of sunrise, and says, ' Sun ! I do this that you may be burning hot, and eat up all the clouds in the sky ! ' [195]

The fires of midwinter have not survived so plainly or so long as those of midsummer. But they have left many traces in connexion with the yule-log,[196] which has survived to this day in England, France, Germany, and some other parts of Europe. The bringing in of the log was a matter of some solemnity, and there were many curious details connected with the burning of it. Thus the log was often lighted with the fragments of last year's log, kept for the purpose. In some places a huge log of oak was fitted into the floor of the hearth, where it slowly charred away during the year, and actually sufficed to light its successor. Sometimes the ash of the old log was strewed upon the fields during the twelve days after Christmas, and this was supposed to promote fertility. In many cases the log was thought to guard the house against witchcraft and against lightning. There are instances where it was regarded as necessary to kindle the log by the friction of wood. There can be no doubt that all these details point to a ritual fire in midwinter corresponding to that of mid-summer, but in later days the fire is generally in the house instead of the open, and therefore the festival has acquired a less public and a more domestic character.

Among the Celtic peoples the principal fire-festivals appear to have been on May Day, or May Eve, and on Hallowe'en, the eve of All Saints' Day. It is curious that these dates have no direct reference to the solstices or to the equinoxes. But they divide the year into equal halves, and they may be said to represent the beginning and the end of the sunnier part of the year : they practically usher in summer and winter. It seems probable that they have a pastoral rather than an agricultural signifi-cance, for the dates roughly represent those times in the year when the herdsman drives out his cattle into the pastures, and when he drives them back again into the fold. It looks as if there was a division of the year based upon the beginning of summer and the beginning of winter, among a pastoral people, which is more primitive than the division according to the solstices.[197]

The Beltane fires, as they were called, on the first of May, were kept up in some parts of England, and more generally in the Highlands of Scotland, until at any rate about the end of the eighteenth century.[198] A traveller in Scotland described the custom as in full force in the Highlands in 1769.[199] In Ireland it appears to have lasted well into the nineteenth century.[200] The fires were kindled upon hill-tops, a trench being previously cut around the site. All the fires in the country-side were put out the night before. The Beltane fire was kindled by the primitive method of boring a hole in a plank of wood and revolving a wooden spindle rapidly in this hole until sparks appeared, which were then used to kindle some special kind of tinder. When the bonfire was alight the company prepared victuals and feasted, and then danced and sang around the flames.[201]

A very interesting and important detail survived in connexion with the Beltane fire at Callander. A cake of oatmeal was baked at the fire, and then divided into equal portions, one of which was blackened with charcoal. Then those around the fire drew the pieces out of a receptacle and the person who received the blackened portion was regarded as devoted to the fire, and had to leap through it three times. Elsewhere in Scotland there was actually the pretence of putting the devoted person on the fire, and while the festival was fresh in the memory of the people they affected to speak of him as dead.[202] There could hardly be a more unmistakable trace than this of the earlier practice of human sacrifice in connexion with the Beltane fires.[203]

There can be very little doubt that the practice of human sacrifice in connexion with these fires, commuted as it sometimes was in later days for the burning of an effigy, has had some effect upon the way that the burning of a 'guy' on the occasion of the 5th of November bonfires has persisted so strikingly. In all likelihood both the bonfire and the effigy would have disappeared long since if they had been merely a memorial of Guy Fawkes and the Gunpowder Plot. It is the dim connexion in the popular memory with both the prehistoric fire and the prehistoric sacrifice that has kept the ritual in being for so long.

In many cases the fires had another picturesque accompaniment. An old cart-wheel, or, in some instances, a wooden wheel specially constructed for the purpose, was swathed in straw and other combustible materials, set on fire, and trundled down a hill-side.[204] This was a widespread custom in various parts of Germany and Switzerland on the first Sunday in Lent, or at Easter.[205] As it took place at night, and every village had its own fire-wheel, the whole horizon was alight with whirling discs of fire, and the spectacle must have been really magnificent. Naogeorgus has left us a description of the rite :

'Some others get a rotten Wheele, all worne and cast
    aside
Which covered round about with strawe and tow, they
    closely hide ;

And caryed to some mountaines top, being all with fire
    alight,
They hurle it down with violence, when darke appears the
    night ;
Resembling much the sunne that from the Heavens down
    should fal,
A strange and monstrous sight it seemes, and fearfull to
    them all.'[206]

This particular rite was observed also in our own
land. Probably the last survival of it is the fire-
wheel called the ' clavie ' which is still burned on a
hill at Burghead, Elgin, in December. It is
significant of the prehistoric origin of this custom
that in the making of the ' clavie ' a stone hammer
must be used.[207] This ritual was still kept up, as
the newspapers reported, in 1926. It is supposed to
secure good luck for the fishing during the ensuing
year.

There is another interesting survival that has no
apparent connexion with the fire-festival of midwinter, and yet must derive from the same kind of
primitive cult. That is to say, it evidently belongs
to the range of prehistoric ritual which gathers
around the notion of the sun's declining warmth as
associated with the death of vegetation, and the
sun's increasing heat as associated with the revival
of vegetation. In various parts of England, especially the northern counties, there is a picturesque
custom known as ' The Sword Dance '. It usually
takes place about Christmas or the New Year.[208]
Olaus Magnus describes such a sword dance, but
without any reference to the more significant part
of the drama which usually accompanies it. He
says that it is a dance in which the young men, as

they move about, hold their swords erect, sheathed at first, and later drawn, and then proceed to lay hold of each other's hilts and points, finishing, after a change of figure, by clashing the swords together.[209]

It will be remembered that Scott introduces the sword dance into *The Pirate*, and gives an account of it, as performed in Shetland, in the notes to the novel. In this version St. George of England, St. Andrew of Scotland, St. Patrick of Ireland, St. David of Wales, St. Denys of France, St. James of Spain, and St. Anthony of Italy, are all introduced as brave knights. They all dance, but there is no pretence of fighting, nor any of the significant drama that we find in other versions of the sword dance.

To-day in Northumberland and Durham the sword dancers are called the 'Guisers', and in Scotland the 'Guizards'. In Northumberland the leader used to have a fox's skin over his head, with the tail hanging down behind,[210] and in Cornwall the man who personated the Hobbyhorse wore a representation of a horse's hide.[211] In Scotland and the north of England 'The Bessy' was usually dressed up as an old woman.[212]

It is said that, early in the last century, the sword dance was performed in Yorkshire from St. Stephen's Day to New Year's Day. There were six dancers dressed in white, with ribands on their garments, attended by a fiddler, a youth called 'The Bessy' and another who plays the part of 'The Doctor'. In this case there is the pretence of killing 'The Bessy' and, apparently, of resuscitating him.[213]

In one case a play of this kind was kept up by
children at Whitehaven until about a hundred years
ago.   It was played at Christmas by boys who were
called ' The Mummers '.   They were bedizened with
ribbons, in the usual style, and wore swords.   Among
the characters were Alexander, the King of Egypt
and his son Prince George, and the Doctor.   Alexander and Prince George fight, and the latter falls.
The Doctor resuscitates him, and the play ends with
the death of the King of Egypt.[214]

In Cornwall the play was performed at Christmas.
The players were dressed up in the usual fashion
with ribands and coloured paper, and so forth, and
each carried a drawn sword.   Among the characters
were St. George, the Turkish Knight, Father
Christmas, the Doctor, and the Hobbyhorse.   St.
George and the Turkish Knight fight, and the latter
falls down as dead.   The Doctor resuscitates him.
They fight again, and this time St. George is left for
dead, whereupon the Hobbyhorse capers in and
carries off the body.   The performance ends with a
dance.[215]   In some versions of the play as performed
in Cornwall the King of Egypt and his son are
introduced.

In Northumberland and Durham to-day the sword
dance is kept up by parties of colliers at Christmas.
They usually wear white shirts decorated with
ribbons.   There is a Captain, with a cocked hat and
peacock's feathers in it, and ' The Bessy ', usually
dressed in women's clothes, who acts as a clown.
The six performers are described in the doggerel
verses which are recited as a squire's son, a tailor,
a soldier, a keelman,[216] another who is merely called
' a jolly dog ' who ' likes his grog ', and the Captain,

whose name is ' True Blue '. ' The Bessy ' then
gives an account of himself in the lines :

> ' My mother was burnt for a witch,
> My father was hanged on a tree,
> And it's because I am a fool
> There's nobody meddled wi' me.'

Then comes the dance with swords. It is
described as an elaborate, graceful, and skilled
performance.   Before the dance ends the performers
begin to fight.   A character who is called the Parson
rushes in to make peace, and receives his death-
blow.   The rest walk round him lamenting his
death.   Then comes in the Doctor, who revives the
Parson ; everybody rejoices, and a general dance
ends the performance.[217]

The version of the sword dance which used to be
performed at Ampleforth in Yorkshire was recorded
about twenty years ago, from the lips of two of the
oldest inhabitants of the village, by the late Mr.
Cecil Sharp, and it was performed under his direction
at the King's Theatre, Hammersmith, in July 1921.
The substance of it is as follows : a character known
as ' The King ' comes home from sea, and is per-
suaded by his father to woo a lady called ' The
Queen '.   Then father and son fall out and fight.
Then a man among the spectators is singled out and
surrounded ; a sword dance is performed around
him, and there is a pretence of killing him.   A
doctor is then called in, who restores the dead man
to life, and another dance ends the play.

The extant versions of these plays contain all
sorts of mixed nonsense.   Sometimes they include
songs and allusions that can be definitely dated as

belonging to the seventeenth century or later, as, for example, references to the war with the Dutch, the siege of Gibraltar, and the battle of Waterloo. We would suggest that most of the stock characters —Alexander, the King of Egypt, St. George, and so on—have really descended from the old mystery plays. But the core of the drama is clearly much older than anything mediaeval. The main points in the ritual evidently are the dance with swords, the pretended slaying of a man, and the pretended revival of the dead person. So in Saxony, at the Whitsuntide rite of ' fetching the Wild Man out of the wood ', there is the pretence of killing the Wild Man, and then a performer who personates a Doctor pretends to bring him to life again.[218] It is fairly clear, therefore, that the sword dance is the survival of some winter rite which is parallel to the many rites of spring and summer (such as the one just mentioned), in which there is a personification of the death and revival of vegetation. It has not left so many traces as the similar rites which belong to the earlier periods of the year, but there evidently was such a primitive ritual in the winter as well as in the summer, exactly as there were ritual fires in winter as well as in summer.

Apart from fire festivals altogether, there are one or two details in which the kindling of fire in primitive times has probably left traces upon our children's games. In the earliest days of humanity fire was a precious gift, and the means of kindling it a wonderful discovery, as the legend of Prometheus is enough to remind us. It is quite possible that at first primitive man got fire accidentally, from a forest conflagration caused by lightning, or some such cause, and kept it by maintaining a perpetual fire, without knowing how to rekindle it if it went out. It is said that there were some Australian tribes in modern times who did not know how to kindle fire, and others who did know, but found the process so difficult that they would go many miles to borrow a spark of fire from another tribe rather than attempt to kindle it for themselves.[219]

Obviously the practice of maintaining a perpetual fire as a part of a religious ritual connects with this early necessity of keeping a fire always alight for the use of the tribe, as does also the practice of rekindling such fires, if they do go out, by the most primitive means, even when better methods have long been familiar. Thus there is a provision in the law of Moses that ' fire shall be kept burning upon the altar continually : it shall not go out '.[220] The Lithuanians kept perpetual fires of oak-wood burning in honour of Perkunas, the god of thunder. In ancient Rome the Vestal Virgins guarded a perpetual fire. If the fire went out the Vestal in charge was stripped and flogged by the Pontifex Maximus, and the flame was rekindled by the friction of two pieces of wood from the *felix arbor*, or, according to others, by the rays of the sun, focused by a conical reflector. It is plain, from several striking parallels, that the Vestals represent, in what has become a religious usage, the daughters of the chieftain of the clan, whose duty it was originally to keep a fire alight for the use of the tribe. So in Damaraland the priestess of the perpetual fire is the chief's daughter.[221] It is said that in Calabria to-day the fire in a peasant's house is never allowed to go out, even in the height of summer, unless a death occurs ;

it is the special care of the daughters of the household to maintain the fire, and if it does happen to
die out there is real dismay at the mishap.[222] So
in Peru the sacred flame was entrusted to the
Virgins of the Sun, and if by any neglect it went
out, the event was regarded as a dire calamity.[223]
And somewhat similar examples of a sacred fire,
perpetually maintained, might be quoted from
various other parts of the world.

Now there is an English game in which a lighted
brand is passed from hand to hand by a group of
children, to the accompaniment of the rhyme :

' Jack's alive and in very good health,
If he dies in your hand you must look to yourself.'[224]

There is an exact parallel to this game in France,
where the formula is : ' The little gentleman is still
alive ! ' and in Germany where it is : ' If the fox
dies I get the skin ! ' [225] In each of these games a
burning stick or spill is passed round, and the child
in whose hand it goes out has to pay a forfeit.
There cannot be much doubt that this is a memory
of those early days when fire would be carried from
hut to hut, or in some cases from tribe to tribe, by
means of a burning brand, and when it was quite a
serious mishap to let it die out.

It is also significant, as we have already remarked,
that when one of the sacred fires was accidentally
allowed to go out, it had to be renewed by the most
primitive methods of kindling flame. When it
would have been easy enough to borrow a flame from
numberless fires around, or to kindle it with flint
and steel, it was yet a ritual necessity that the fire
should be kindled by friction between two pieces of

wood, that is to say, by the earliest method known
to man. Thus when one of the perpetual fires
which the Lithuanians kept burning as a part of the
worship of the god Perkunas happened to go out,
it had to be kindled afresh by the friction of two
pieces of oak, that being the wood specially used to
maintain the fires.[226] So the fire on which the
buffalo calf is roasted, at the sacrificial feast which
the Todas in South India celebrate every year, must
be kindled by the rubbing of sticks,[227] though
modern methods of kindling fire are common enough
in the district. It is stated by Montanus that in
early times the perpetual lamps in churches were
lighted by fire made by friction of dry wood. There
is a custom, found in both the Eastern and the
Western Church, of extinguishing all lights in the
churches on Easter Eve, and then secretly kindling
a new flame with a burning-glass or with flint and
steel, from which the great paschal candle is lighted,
which is then used to re-light all the extinguished
lamps in the church.[228] It is noticeable that while
the primitive and laborious way of kindling flame
by the friction of wood has been given up, an
ancient and unusual way of obtaining fire has been
retained. This very ceremony, by the way, took
place annually at Lemnos in the temple of Hephais-
tos, at Rome in that of Vesta, and at Cuzco in that
of the Sun. It is found in other instances also ; for
example, among the Brahmans in India, the Kaffirs
in Africa, and the Chippeways in North America.
In some parts of Swabia the Easter fires might not
be kindled by the usual means, but only by the
friction of wood. The same was true of the midsummer fires in some districts of East Prussia.[229]

Similarly, the Beltane fires in the Highlands of Scotland, down to at least the beginning of the nineteenth century, had to be kindled with *tein-eigin*, that is, need-fire.[230] The process was to turn an oak spindle rapidly in a hole bored in a plank of the same wood until fire was produced.

Now anyone who is familiar with the fire-drills used by some savage peoples—the American Indians, for example—must have been struck by the resemblance between the shape of many of them and the shape of a boy's spinning-top. It has been suggested that the top is developed from the spindle employed in weaving,[231] but it appears to be more likely to be connected with the fire-drill. It is not a very far-fetched suggestion that the spindle of the fire-drill, the very purpose of which was to be twirled around rapidly by the hand, or by a thong, was the origin of this particular toy, and that when a boy spins a top he is in a direct line of descent from primitive man twirling his fire-drill to produce flame.

CHAPTER V

FAIRIES AND GOBLINS

THE widespread game of *Tag, Tig,* or *Tiggy* has developed many forms, but the essence of it is that one player runs after the others, and if he can touch any of them, the one who is touched becomes in his turn the pursuer. The interesting point, however, is that a player cannot be ' tigged ' under certain conditions, as, in one variant of the game, when squatting, but more generally when touching wood, or, in all the primitive forms of the game, when touching iron.

This last is said to have been the universal form of the game in the United States in earlier times, and it is still played in that way in some places. It seems to have been the one form of the game originally in England, for a writer in the *Gentleman's Magazine* in the middle of the eighteenth century says that in former times ' *Tag* was all the play, where the lad saves himself by touching of cold iron '.[232] It is called in various parts of Germany and Switzerland *Eisen anfassen* or *Eisenzech* or *Eisenziggi*, and in Italy *Toccaferro*.[233]

One formula for the game in Germany is :

> ' Dreimal eiserne Stangen,
> Wer nicht läuft wird gefangen,
> Dreimal eiserne Schnitz,
> Wer nicht läuft wird gesitzt,
> Dreimal über den Rhein,
> Wer nicht läuft ist mein.'[234]

(' One, two, three, an iron post,
Unless you run away, you're lost.
One, two, three, an iron bar,
Unless you run both fast and far—
One, two, three, across the Rhine,
You're a prisoner of mine ! ')

The pursuer in the game, as it was played in Lincolnshire, was known as ' Horney ', obviously, like Burns's Auld Hornie, the Devil.[235] Similarly it is a witch who seizes a child in a German game *Die Hexe kommt*.[236] But the very fact that iron is a protecting charm in the game is enough to show that in the original conception the pursuer is regarded as some unearthly creature, such as a demon, a witch, or a fairy, for, as an old writer puts it, ' all uncouth, unknown wights are terrified by nothing earthly so much as cold iron '.[237]

The reason for this general conviction that iron is dreaded by fairies, witches, demons, and the like is a very interesting one. In the first place it is beyond all reasonable doubt that the widespread belief in fairies, elves, gnomes, and such-like creatures, originated in the contact between a dwarfish race of primitive habits and a taller people more advanced in the arts of life. Such a contact did take place in our own land, and such collisions must have taken place many times in many countries. Imagine a small, feeble folk, who live in caves and burrows beneath the ground, and who are armed only with stone, coming into conflict with a taller, stronger people who live in huts (and therefore regard the underground dwellings of the little folk as strange and unnatural) and who are armed with iron. The small people with their flint weapons will dread these new, strange, terrible weapons of metal, and fly from them.   Consequently it is certain that the legendary lore of the more advanced race will be full of stories of a little people who live under the earth, who have stone weapons, and who are terrified of iron.   It is equally certain that they will be credited with unearthly powers, and presently classed with wizards, goblins, and demons, for almost all primitive races are credited with supernatural powers by their superiors and conquerors ; so, for example, the Swedes regard the Lapps, and the Singalese regard the Veddahs, as adepts in wizardry.   There can be no doubt that with the lapse of the ages, and especially with the spread of Christianity, all the objects of ancient dread—the old gods, now regarded as demons, the primitive races, now regarded as fairies, gnomes, and trolls, and all those credited with supernatural powers, as witches and wizards, were all mingled together in one range of superstition, as uncanny creatures ; and the fear of Christian symbols and the dread of iron, along with other primitive traits that belonged to one or other of them, were extended to all.[238]

The fairies have all the traits that we know were possessed by some of these very primitive races which were later dispossessed by more advanced races of larger physical development.   All the stories represent the fairies as small folk who live beneath the ground, and who are afraid of iron, along with several other significant attributes that really belong to a primitive race of men—they are heathen who lived long before the coming of Christ, they have only a very rudimentary notion of number, and so on. There is any amount of evidence of all this.

Thus the fairies generally are ' the little people ', and when any fairy is particularly described this smallness of stature is usually emphasized. Oberon, the king of the fairies, is only three feet in height, as we learn from the romance of Huon of Bordeaux, and many of his subjects, as is only proper, are much smaller, some of them not more than a foot high. In folk-tales about fairies the diminutive stature is nearly always mentioned.[239] To give only a few examples, the fairy who came to steal a fisherwoman's newly born baby in Scotland is described as ' a little man dressed in green ',[240] and the fairies who surrounded a man at the Llorfa in Wales are described as ' little beings like men '.[241] So Drayton writes, in the *Poet's Elysium*, of one of his feminine elves :

> ' Why, by her smallness you may find
> That she is of the fairy kind.'

Sometimes it is the extreme smallness of a child that first betrays it as being of the fairy race. There was a fairy changeling in Mecklenburg ' who was no bigger than a shoe at two years old ',[242] and this was plain proof of its elfin character.

The fairies are also consistently described as living underground. As an old writer on the supernatural tells us : ' The faeries do principally inhabit the mountains and caverns of the earth.' [243] In Scandinavia some of the fairies were known as Bjergfolk, or hill-people, and in Germany as Haulemännerchen, or little cave-men.[244] When mortals visit the fairies it is never a building above

6

ground in which they are found, but always some mysterious entrance is discovered opening into a hill-side. In the English folk-tale it is from the fairy mound that Childe Rowland rescues his imprisoned sister, Burd Ellen, who has been carried off by the elf. Similarly in a Gaelic story it is from the fairy hillock that a woman carried off by the fairies is rescued by her husband, who secures an entrance by using iron and a black cock.²⁴⁵ And so in all the stories. The barrows in which pre-historic men buried their dead are regarded as fairy mounds in Denmark, in Holland, and in other lands.²⁴⁶

Another very interesting characteristic which the fairies share with very primitive races of men is that they have only the simplest elements of number. It has been pointed out that there is only one Welsh fairy (one is irresistibly reminded of Falstaff and Sir Hugh Evans : 'Heavens defend me from that Welsh fairy !') who is represented as counting, and she counts by *fives*. She is a fairy bride who is promised as a dowry as many sheep, cattle, goats, and horses as she can count without drawing breath, and she says : ' Un, dau, tri, pedwar, pump ; un, dau, tri, pedwar, pump ' (' One, two, three, four, five ; one, two, three, four, five '), as fast as her tongue can go.²⁴⁷ Now the earliest races of men had only learned to count on the fingers of one hand, and consequently quinary numeration is the most primitive kind of counting. There are what look like faint traces of the preference for counting by fives in other stories. In a Danish tale a charm has to be uttered *fifteen* times ²⁴⁸ to make the elves come out of the hill; and in an Irish tale the midwife who has been to the help of the queen of the fairies is rewarded with *five* pieces of gold, which presently turn into five withered oak-leaves.[249]

Then, too, fairies are thought of as belonging to the heathen world, long before the advent of Christianity.[250] They ' were of the old profession ' in a remoter sense than good Bishop Corbet ever dreamt. In Cornwall the fairies are believed to be the spirits of the people who lived long ago, ages before the coming of Christ, and who were too good to be doomed to hell, and not good enough to be taken to heaven. There is a similar belief in Ireland. One quaint variation of this notion, found in both Wales and Cornwall, is that the fairies are the ancient Druids who have become smaller and smaller because they would not give up their idolatry.[251] Among the peasantry in Devon the pixies are believed to be the souls of infants who died before they were baptized.[252] But whatever form the fancy takes, the fairies are always thought of as somehow pre-Christian or un-Christian.

Sometimes they dislike all Christian usages, and vanish at an invocation of the name of God. Thus a woman in Shetland once saw a fairy sitting by her hearth. She asked him who he was, and he answered, ' I am Trippa's son.' She *sained* herself (i.e. invoked a blessing on herself) and he instantly vanished.[253] The gnomes in the Cornish mines object to the sign of the cross ; a man who made a cross on the rock in one of the levels to mark his way back was compelled to alter it by the miners, manifestly on this ground.[254] The Scandinavian trolls particularly dislike church bells. A troll who lived on a hill at Botna in Sweden was disgusted

when bells were hung in the church there, and
said :

> ' In Botna-hill 'twas good to dwell
> Before they hung that wretched bell ! '

So in Denmark a disconsolate troll told a farmer that
he was leaving the country, as he could not bear
the everlasting ringing of the church bells.[255]

Sometimes, on the other hand, knowing themselves
to be beyond the Christian pale, they are pathetically
anxious about their chance of salvation. In Denmark a clergyman was journeying past a hill where
there was music and merriment. Some dwarfs
suddenly sprang out of it, and asked him if he
thought they could be saved. He said that he
could not answer so momentous a question at once,
but he would give them an answer in a year's time.
When he passed again a year later they asked the
same question, and he said, ' No, you are all lost ! '
Instantly the whole hill seemed to burst into flame.
Another form of the legend makes a Neck ask the
question, and the priest says, ' No : sooner shall
this staff in my hand bud and blossom than that
thou shalt be saved ! ' The elf wept, and the priest
went on his way. But soon the staff began to put
forth leaves and blossoms (as in the legend of
Tannhäuser) and the priest went back to tell the
Neck, who rejoiced greatly, and played joyously on
his harp all night long.[256]

Again, like many primitive races, the fairies
possess only stone weapons. The prehistoric arrow-
heads of flint found in the soil are called by the
peasantry ' elf-darts '. The country people in
Ireland still believe, on some occasions when their

cattle are sick, that they have been ' elf-shot ' ; [257] the wise man called in to help will show a dent in the animal's flesh where the arrow struck, and a sovereign remedy is water in which a flint arrow-head has been steeped. It was believed that the ' elf arrow-heads ' were sometimes found sticking in the clothing of people who had been shot at by the fairies. The supernatural character of these stone weapons was also indicated in the belief that they could not be found by looking for them, but only chanced upon ; and by the conviction that, when found, they should be kept in the dark, or the fairies might find them again and use them for evil. [258]

And finally the fairies are afraid of iron. So are goblins, demons, witches, and all uncanny creatures, for they all belong in some way to the same dim under-world. Iron is a defence against the jinn among the Arabs, [259] and against the demons among the Indians, [260] and indeed against evil spirits in every part of the world. The witches in Germany are powerless against you if you stand on a key, a chain, or a harrow, which are all of iron. [261] In Scotland the fairies have no power over you if you have a knife or a nail on your person. [262]

The folk-tales abound with illustrations of this belief about iron. In Wales one way of getting rid of the fairy changeling is to put it on the floor and let all the people in the house throw a piece of iron at it. [263] A piece of iron in the hand of a blacksmith is often a sovereign weapon against such creatures. In Denmark a troll was driving off a woman when a smith heard her lamenting, and springing out with a red-hot iron in his hand, held it between the troll and his captive, whereupon he had to abandon her.[264] In exactly the same way a smith rushed out with a red-hot iron in his hand and rescued Nancy Trenoweth, a girl in Cornwall, who was being carried off by a spectral bridegroom.[265] In Wales, when a young man had got into a fairy ring and had been carried off to fairyland, he was rescued after a year and a day, when he was found again dancing with the fairies in the ring, touched with a piece of iron, and dragged out.[266] So in innumerable folk-tales iron is used to prevent pursuit by these creatures, or to secure escape from their dwellings, when a mortal has visited them. The midwife in Denmark casts a knife behind her when she leaves the troll's house laden with gifts, and the father in Scotland sticks his dirk into the threshold when he enters the fairy hill to recover his son.[267]

Sometimes the touch of iron will send back a fairy, or one who has been in the power of the fairies, to fairyland. So a servant girl who had been taken by the fairies was rescued, after a year and a day, and told her master that she would stay with him until he struck her with iron. One day, helping to harness a horse, she was struck with the bit, and disappeared.[268] A whole cycle of tales gathers around this last detail. In many of them a man marries a fairy bride who consents to live with him as long as he does not strike her with iron. One day, when he is in a hurry, by the merest accident, he taps her with something of iron, and the mischief is done. In one story the husband and wife went into the field to catch the pony. The fairy wife was nimbler than her husband, and getting her hand in the pony's mane, called to him to throw her a

halter. He threw a bridle with an iron bit, which
unluckily struck her. She flew away at once, and
plunged into the Lake of Corwrion, whence she came
at first.[269]

All this quaint evidence goes to prove that the
game of *Tag* is originally based upon the notion of
pursuit by some creature such as a demon, a goblin,
or a fairy, in which the person pursued saves himself
by the power of iron.

There are other children's games which connect
with the same unearthly creatures by way of a
different detail. For there are some games which
depend for their climax upon the ability of the child
to restrain himself (in the face of some suggestion
toward it) from laughing, or betraying astonishment, and there are other games that end in a
pretended sneeze. In the game of *Buff* a child with
a stick thumps it on the ground, and the dialogue
ensues :

> ' Knock ! knock ! '
> ' Who's there ? '
> ' Buff.'
> ' What says Buff ? '
> ' Buff says Buff to all his men,
>   And I say Buff to you again.'
> ' Methinks Buff smiles ! '
> ' Buff neither laughs nor smiles,
> ⸢But looks in your face
>   With a comical grace,
>   And delivers the staff to you again.'[270]

If he goes through the ordeal without laughing,
another player has to take his place. So in Germany
a child carrying a staff, and known as *Father Eber-
hard*, stands in the midst of a circle of children and

strikes one of them with his staff, whereupon the
one indicated steps out and says :

> ' Vater Eberhard,
> Ich fasse dich an deinem ehrwürdigen Bart.
> Wenn du mich wirst sehen lachen
> Werd ich an deiner Stelle wachen.'[271]

> (' Father Eberhard,
> I pull your reverend beard,
> If I laugh, or make a face,
> I will come and take your place.')

Another German game has the formula :

> ' Ich bin der Herr von Rech,
> Verbiete Lach und Sprech :
> War lacht und spricht
> Ein Pfand verbricht.'[272]

> (' The Herr von Rech am I,
> I forbid you to laugh or to cry :
> If you speak or laugh, I say,
> That a forfeit you must pay.')

So in America the game of *The Staff* [273] (which is
like *Buff*) turns wholly upon the player going
through a ritual without laughing. The game of
Club Fist [274] ends with the proclamation : ' The
first who laughs, or grins, or shows his teeth, has
three pinches and three knocks ! ' In Germany
there is an almost exact parallel :

> ' Gugelhöpfli,
> Ufem Töpfli,
> Wer lächelt, wer schmützlet,
> Wer d' Zähnli füre leht,
> Der muess es Pfand ge.'[275]

> (' If you laugh, or if you grin,
> Or show your teeth above your chin—
> A forfeit you must pay ! ')

The game of *Ring-a-Ring-o'-Roses* is played with
the formula :

> ' Ring-a-ring-o'-roses !
> A pocket full o' posies,
> One for me, one for you,
> And one for little Moses.
> A-tisha, a-tisha, a-tisha ! '[276]

The last words indicate, of course, an explosion of
pretended sneezing.

Now there is a notion in the primitive mind that
laughing, yawning, sneezing, and so on, have a close
connexion with the human spirit.[277] The thought
seems to be originally that when you do any of these
things your spirit may escape in the act, and another
spirit may seize the chance of entering your body,
or gaining some power over you. Hence the widespread custom of blessing anyone who sneezes. The
Greeks said ' Ζεῦ σώσον ! ' the Romans said ' Salve ! '
the Jews said ' Asuta ! ' (' Health ! ') or ' Hayyim
tobim ! ' (' for a happy life ! '), the Germans ' Gott
hilf ! ' the Italians ' Felicità ! ' the English ' God
bless you ! ' whenever anyone sneezed. There are
innumerable references to the prevalence of this
custom all over the world. Thus there is an epigram
in the Greek Anthology on a man who could not
wipe his nose, because his nose was longer than his
arm, and who did not say ' God save us ! ' when he
sneezed, because his nose was so far from his ears
that he could not hear the sneeze.[278] To-day the
Greek says, when anyone sneezes, ' Health to thee,
and joy to thee ! ' (Γειὰ σου καὶ χαρά σου') and
sometimes adds, as a supreme expression of good
wishes, ' And may thy mother-in-law burst ! '[279]
In Caxton's edition of *The Golden Legend* the custom

is given an entirely fictitious explanation. We are told that it derived from a pestilence at Rome when sneezing was a premonition of death, ' so that when any person was herd snesyng, anone they that were by said to hym, God helpe you, or Cryst helpe, and yet endureth the custome. And also when he sneseth or gapeth he maketh to fore his face the signe of the crosse and blessith hym '.[280] In the *Homilies* there is a passage discouraging the use of ' these sayings : such as neese, God help and Saint John ! ' and several other invocations of saints.[281] A similar practice is found in savage countries to-day. When anyone sneezes in Tonga the bystanders say ' Ofa ', which means ' Love '. In Samoa they say ' Soefua ', which is equivalent to ' God bless you ! '[282] When the Sultan of Dafur coughs every one at Court must make a hissing sound ; when he sneezes, every one must utter a sound like the cry of a jeko.[283]

The same sort of notion obtained as to yawning. Thus the Moslems bless themselves when they yawn, for the Devil is in the habit of leaping into a gaping mouth. So the Hausa utters a prayer after yawning, hiccoughing, or sneezing.[284] A Kruman in Africa lay all night with his nose and mouth tied up to prevent the escape of his soul, because he had had a dream which he knew was meant to draw his soul away in the night.[285] In Transylvania it is thought that a child ought not to sleep with his mouth open, not on hygienic grounds, but because the soul may slip out in the shape of a mouse, and then the child will never waken again.[286] In West Timor a man holds his right hand before his mouth when he is speaking, lest a demon should enter his body, and lest the person with whom he converses should harm the speaker's soul by magic.[287] Our custom of putting the hand before the mouth when yawning goes back to the same sort of conception.

Sometimes the sneeze or the yawn is regarded as an omen, good or bad. When Telemachus sneezed loudly, so that the roof rang, Penelope said to Eumaeus the swineherd : ' Dost thou not mark how my son has sneezed a blessing on my words ? '[288] The modern Greek regards a sneeze by a listener as a confirmation of what has just been said by anyone who is speaking.[289] Xenophon relates that when he was addressing the Ten Thousand at a critical juncture in the campaign one of the soldiers near him happened to sneeze. The whole army shouted the usual invocation to Zeus, and Xenophon, seizing upon the omen, proposed a solemn vow to offer sacrifice in the first friendly country they reached. All united in the vow, and shouted the paean.[290] The Zulu regards sneezing as fortunate, for it is his ancestral spirit present with him that makes him sneeze. In some parts of England it was thought lucky to sneeze early in the day, for it meant that you would hear good news or receive a gift.[291] In the Greek Anthology there is an epigram in which a sneeze is evidently regarded as an omen, for it relates that a man sneezed near a tomb, and then hoped to hear news of his wife's death. He also sneezed to the winds (ἔπταρον εἰς ἀνέμους), but in vain, for neither illness nor death came to her.[292] A sneeze is both a good and a bad omen in the child's rhyme :

> ' Sneeze on Monday, sneeze for danger,
> Sneeze on Tuesday, kiss a stranger,

Sneeze on Wednesday, get a letter,
Sneeze on Thursday, something better,
Sneeze on Friday, sneeze for sorrow,
Sneeze on Saturday, see your true love to-morrow.'[293]

St. Augustine condemns, among other superstitious practices, that of returning to bed if anyone sneezes when you are putting on your slippers, where the omen was clearly regarded as unlucky.[294] A cacique of the Abipones refused the Spanish governor's offer of a pinch of snuff, of which he was usually very fond, because his wife had just had a baby, explaining his refusal by saying : ' What a danger my sneezing would bring upon my child ! ' [295] In New Zealand a charm was uttered to prevent evil when a child sneezed. The Basques believe that sometimes a witch carries away a child who is not blessed when it sneezes.[296] It used to be thought in Scotland that a newly-born child was in the fairy spell until it sneezed : then all danger was past. An old nurse (who had been taking snuff at the very moment and thereby no doubt assisted the good omen) exclaimed joyfully when the baby sneezed, ' God sain the bairn, it's no' a warlock ! ' [297] So it was believed in this country that an adult who sneezed was liable to be carried off by the fairies unless some one said ' God bless you ! ' It is significant that at the end of the frenzied Bori dance among the Hausa (in which the performers get into a state of hysteria and do all kinds of violence to themselves without feeling it) the dancer sneezes, and this expels the spirit by which he has been possessed.[298] When the prophet restored the Shunamite's son to life, ' the child sneezed seven times, and opened his eyes '.[299]

There was an uncanny significance also in laughing. It is illustrated by a queer detail in the ritual of the Lupercalia in ancient Rome. Plutarch tells us that after the sacrifice was completed the Luperci were touched on the forehead with the bloody knife that had slain the goats. The bloodstain was wiped off with wool dipped in milk, and then the two youths had to *laugh*. This may be the symbol of a return to life after the pretence of a sacrificial death, or it may indicate a possession by the god.[300] It has been pointed out that the former view is supported by the description given by Pausanias of what happened to those who visited the famous oracle in the cave of Trophonius at Lebadeia in Boeotia. In a most interesting account of the rites (at first hand, for Pausanias says, ' I write not from mere hearsay ; I have myself consulted Trophonius '), he tells us that after a man has visited the cave, he is taken in hand by the priests, and questioned as to all he saw and heard there. Then they hand him over to his friends, and he is taken to the house of Good Fortune and the Good Demon, where he lodged before, being still unconscious of himself and of his surroundings. ' Afterward, however,' says Pausanias, ' he will have all his wits as before, and *the power of laughter* will come back to him.' [301]

Now there is a very widespread superstition concerning changelings, which survived in our own land down to very recent days. The fairies steal a human child, and leave one of their own in its place.[302] The reason for this is not very clear. It was believed in Ireland that the fairies carried off the children of mortals for sacrifice, as they have to offer one to the Devil every seven years.[303] In a

Welsh tale the motive is cannibalism. The fairy who rejoiced in the name of Canrig the Stumpy was discovered eating a baby by the man who had been sent to destroy her.[304]

The fairy child who is left in the place of the stolen infant is known to be a changeling because it is uncanny in several ways—it is often very small, and does not grow up ; it has an abnormal appetite ; it screams and cries continually ; or it is up to some unnatural mischief. One of the best ways to prove that it is a changeling, and to get rid of it, is to make it laugh, or sneeze, or, by some fantastic performance, to astonish it into revealing itself as unearthly by confessing that it is very old. So with a changeling in Germany. A wise neighbour tells the mother to set the changeling down on the hearth and boil some water in two egg-shells, which will make him laugh, ' and *if he laughs* it will be all over with him '. The changeling watches the process, and exclaims : ' I am as old as the Westerwald, but never yet have I seen anyone boil anything in an egg-shell ! ' Then he begins to laugh, and suddenly a host of little elves appear, who bring the right child back, and take the changeling away with them.[305] There was a proverbial phrase in Germany, ' To laugh like a kobold ', and another, ' You laugh as though you'd empty yourself, like a kobold '.[306] Though it seems to look in the opposite direction it probably belongs to the same range of ideas when in the Norse version of the tale of *Snow-white and Rosy-red*, the old queen declares that the dumb heroine must be a witch, because she could ' neither talk, nor *laugh*, nor weep '.[307]

In other stories of this type the detail of laughter

does not appear, and all the emphasis is on the fairies' amazement at the astonishing act. In Mecklenburg it is told that the fairies had stolen a child, and, according to their usual custom, had left a changeling in place of it. The mother was advised by an old man to pour new beer into an empty egg-shell, and proceed to ferment it with yeast. The imp watched with astonishment, and said :

> ' I am as old
> As Bohemian gold,
> Yet never saw what I see here,
> An egg-shell used for brewing beer ! '[308]

The same night he disappeared. Similarly in one Welsh tale the woman used an egg-shell to boil the pottage, and in another to make a pasty, in each case for the dinner of the reapers.[309] In Normandy several egg-shells are used, and the changeling says : ' Seven times have I seen the Forest of Ardennes burnt, but I never saw so many pots boil ! ' In Brittany milk is boiled in several egg-shells, and the astounded changeling exclaims (with some delightful autobiographical detail that one could wish expanded) : ' I shall soon be a hundred years old, but I never saw so many shells boiling ! I was born in Pif and in Paf, in the country where the cats are made, and I never saw anything like it ! ' [310] In all these examples the astonishment is enough to make the changeling depart. There is a Gaelic story of this type where the fairies had taken the child and left a changeling, and a poor woman told the mother what to do. She followed the instructions, and made a circle of eggs on the floor. ' What are you doing in that manner ? ' said the changeling,

sullenly. ' I am making a brewing cauldron ', she
said. ' A brewing cauldron ? ' said he. ' I am
more than three hundred years old, and I never yet
saw a brewing cauldron like that ! ' This showed
that the child was a changeling, but she had to get
rid of him in this case by looking out of the window
and saying that she saw Torr-a-Bhuilg on fire,
whereupon he sprang out of the door, saying :
' My hammers and my anvil and my bellows ! ' and
was never seen again.[311]

But the detail of laughing, sneezing, or yawning
appears to be primitive in these stories, and though
it has disappeared from many, it still remains in
some. So in an Esthonian tale which does not
concern a changeling, but a fairy who had been
captured by a man, had lived for years amongst
human folk, and had finally become the wife of the
captor's son. One day she burst out laughing in
church. It was because she saw the Devil writing
on a horseskin stretched on the wall of the church
the names of those who slept or gossiped during
service. He filled up all the space on the skin, and
then pulled it with his teeth to stretch it out. In
doing this he bumped his head against the wall,
and made a grimace. It was this that had made her
laugh. She would only tell her husband the reason
of her mirth on condition that he told her how she
had come to his father's house at first. He told
her the secret, and she took advantage of it to
disappear.[312]

Sometimes it is a yawn that is the betraying
detail. In Iceland the troll who has transformed
herself into a lovely queen says : ' When I yawn a
little yawn, I am a little maiden ; when I yawn a

half-yawn, then I am as a half-troll ; when I yawn a whole yawn then am I as a whole troll ! ' [313] Or it may be a sneeze that gives the fairy away. Thus in an Irish tale of a changeling it is a woman with the ' evil eye ' who has changed the child. The mother watches for the woman, and cuts off a piece of her cloak. This is burned close to the child and the smoke makes him sneeze, when the spell is broken and the mother's own child is restored.[314] And so in respect of human beings who have been bewitched, and changed into another form. Thus a folk-tale relates that a man often met, in going through a wood, an adder which always sneezed thrice as it passed him. He consulted the priest, and was advised to say : ' God help thee ! ' as he would to a man. He did so once, but then lost his nerve and ran away. A similar tale tells that a man heard some one sneeze as he passed through the forest, but could see nobody. He said : ' God help thee ! ' There was a second sneeze, and again he said : ' God help thee ! ' The sneeze was repeated a third time, and, losing patience, he exclaimed : ' Oh, go to the devil ! ' Then a mannikin appeared, and said sadly : ' If you had said a third time, " God help thee ! " I should have been delivered.' Then he added (and the snake in the first tale said precisely the same thing) that he must now wait until an acorn had fallen from one of the trees, and grown into an oak, and had been felled, and a cradle had been made of the timber, and then a child rocked in that cradle would be able to deliver him.[315] There is a precise parallel to this detail in the cry of our English brownie, *The Cauld Lad of Hylton*, who says :

7

'Wae's me ! wae's me !
The acorn's not fallen from the tree,
That's to grow the wood,
That's to make the cradle,
That's to rock the bairn,
That's to lay me ! '[316]

In the other stories, however, the significant point is that the sneeze indicates that the adder and the mannikin are human beings who are bewitched, or in the power of the fairies, and that only a threefold blessing in the name of God can deliver them.

There cannot be much doubt that games like *Buff* and *Dump* and *Ring-a-Ring-o'-Roses*, in which a laugh or a sneeze is the climax, originated in this range of quaint notions as to the uncanny significance of laughing and sneezing, and the betrayal, or the danger, or the deliverance, which these things may indicate.

CHAPTER VI

FOUNDATIONS AND SACRIFICES

ONE of the most familiar of our children's games is *London Bridge is Broken Down*. Two players form an arch with uplifted hands ; the rest pass through, each holding on to the one before, and hurrying to get past in safety. The last is caught by the descending arms of the first two players. Sometimes this is repeated until all the children have been caught and placed on the right or the left, and the game ends with a tug of war.

The formula varies somewhat, but this is a representative version :

> ' London Bridge is broken down,
> Broken down, broken down,
> London Bridge is broken down,
> My fair lady ! '

> ' How shall we build it up again,
> Up again, up again,
> How shall we build it up again ?
> My fair lady ! '

> ' Build it up with stone and lime . . .'
> ' Stone and lime would wash away . . .'
> ' Built it up with iron bars . . .'
> ' Iron bars would bend and break . . .'
> ' Build it up with gold and silver . . .'
> ' Gold and silver would be stole away . . .'
> ' Get a watch to watch all night . . .'
> ' Suppose the watch should fall asleep ? . . .'

' Get a dog to bark all night . . .'
' Suppose the dog should get a bone ? . . .'
' Get a cock to crow all night . . .'
' Suppose the cock should fly away ? . . .'
' What has this poor prisoner done ? . . .'
' Robbed a house and killed a man . . .'
' What will you take to set him free ? . . .'
' A hundred pounds will set him free . . .'
' A hundred pounds he has not got . . .'
' Then off to prison he must go,
  My fair lady ! '[317]

Now the mediaeval London Bridge, which was
the work of Isembert the Frenchman, whom King
John brought over the sea to build it, was once
actually broken down, in the reign of Henry III.
This happened because the King had granted the
bridge revenues to his Queen, Eleanor of Provence,
and they were squandered by her instead of being
expended on the maintenance of the bridge.   It has
been suggested that the game and the rhyme derive
from that collapse of London Bridge in the thirteenth
century.

That cannot be, however, for the game is mentioned in earlier times, and occurs in many different
countries.   Naturally the bridge has been differently
localized.   In England it is always *London Bridge*,
as one would expect, for that was not only for long
centuries the one great bridge in the metropolis,
but it must have been for many generations the
most considerable bridge in the whole country.   In
Scotland the bridge has no local habitation—the
game is merely *Broken Bridges Falling Down*.[318]
In New England it is *Charlestown Bridge*,[319] which
was built as recently as 1786.   In France, again, it
is not localized ; it is merely *Le Pont-Levis*. Rabelais

mentions it as one of Gargantua's games, under the
name *Aux ponts chus, Fallen Bridges.*[320] In some
parts of Germany it is merely *Die goldene Brücke.*
In other parts it is *Die Magdeburger Brücke,* or *Die
Meissner Brücke.* In Aargau it is *d'holländische
Brugg*—a form which has survived amongst the
Germans in the United States. In Danzig it is
(again in dialect) *de gröne Bröck* (' the Green Bridge ')
being the bridge over the Mottlau by the Green
Tower.[321] But in nearly all these forms the
essential parts of the game are preserved—the
bridge is falling down, there are suggestions that it
should be rebuilt in this way or that, and the
climax of the game is the seizure of a captive, who
is often a malefactor.

In the French game *Le Pont-Levis* the two tallest
of the players make a raised drawbridge with their
lifted arms, and the rest pass through, the last being
seized. The words are :

> ' Trois fois passera,
> La dernière, la dernière ;
> Trois fois passera,
> La dernière y restera.'[322]
>
> (' Three times pass by—
> The last, the last, I say ;
> Three times pass by—
> And here the last must stay ! ')

This is practically the same as the game called
La Porte du Gloria,[323] where the two leading players
are called ' The Sun ' and ' The Moon '. The game
called *Olivé Beauvé* is evidently another variant of
the game of fallen bridges. One of the leaders of
the game has the title part, and is followed by a

line of children. The other leader is called *La Voisine*. She advances toward Olivé Beauvé, with the words :

> ' Que tu as de jolies filles ! Olivé Beauvé ;
> Que tu as de jolies filles !
> Sur le pont-chevalier.'

Then Olivé Beauvé answers to the effect that they are prettier children than the neighbour's, and she asks for one of them.   Then Olivé Beauvé says :

> ' Je la donne, *si tu l'attrapes*,
> Olivé Beauvé ;
> Je la donne, *si tu l'attrapes*
> Sur le pont-chevalier.'[324]

> (' How many pretty girls you have,
> Olivé Beauvé ;
> How many pretty daughters,
> On the bridge across the waters !

> ' *Seize her*, and I will give you one,
> Olivé Beauvé ;
> One of my pretty daughters,
> On the bridge across the waters ! ')

Then the neighbour attempts to seize one of the children, is baffled for a time, but finally succeeds. The game continues until all the children have been seized, and then *La Voisine* and *Olivé Beauvé* change places, and it recommences.   The mention of the bridge, *Le Pont Chevalier* (which we venture to suggest may be a corruption of *Le Pont Chevalé*—' the propped-up bridge ') and the seizure of the children, is enough to establish the game in the succession of games of the type of *London Bridge is Broken Down*.

Olivé Beauvé closely resembles another French game, the ronde *Giroflé girofla* :

> ' Que t'as de belles filles ?
> Giroflé, girofla,
> Que t'as de belles filles ?
> L'amour m'y compt'ra.
>
> Donnez-moi z'en donc une ?
> Giroflé, girofla,
> Donnez-moi z'en donc une ?
> L'amour m'y compt'ra.'[325]

> (' You have many pretty girls—
> (Gillyflowers are fine !)
> You have many pretty girls—
> Love will keep them mine.
>
> Will you give me one of them ?
> (Gillyflowers are fine !)
> Will you give me one of them ?
> Love will keep them mine.')

This game introduces the King and the Queen, and finally the Devil. In the German game of *Die goldene Brücke* the formula is :

> ' Kann ich wol über die goldene Brücke ? '
> ' Nein, sie ist entzwei gebrochen.'
> ' Wer hat sie entzwei gebrochen ? '
> ' Der König, der König mit seiner jüngsten Tochter.'
> ' Ich werde sie wieder machen lassen.'
> ' Womit ? '
> ' Mit Perlenring und goldenem Stein,'
> ' Was giebst du mir zum Pfande ? '
> ' Den hintesten, den du kriegen kannst.'[326]

(' " May I go over the Golden Bridge ? " " No, it is broken down." " Who has broken it ? " " The King, the King, and his youngest daughter." " I will build it up again." "How?" "With rings of pearl and stones of gold." "What will you give me for a forfeit?" "The hindermost one that you can get".')

Then one of the players is seized.

Now there has been, almost all over the world, a custom of offering a human sacrifice on laying the foundation of a building. This is first of all a propitiation of the spirits of the earth, who are being disturbed ; later on it sometimes passes into another conception—the ghost of the victim will be a spectral guard of the building that is erected. But in the first significance it is a sacrifice to the earth-spirits, or, in the case of a bridge, to the water-spirits. There is an enormous mass of evidence as to the existence of the rite, and it is easy to trace the gradual fashion in which its darkest features passed away. The actual rite has been witnessed by Europeans in savage lands. Eighty years or so ago an English sailor in Fiji saw men buried alive in the holes in which the posts of the chief's house were being set up.[327] So in Siam when a new gate was being erected in the wall of a town the builders would lie in wait and seize the first passers-by, who were buried alive under the gate-posts.[328] And similarly in many savage lands.

There are many traces of it in European legends. Thus, when Romulus founded Rome, Faustulus and Quinctilius were slain and buried in a deep pit under a huge stone. In our own land the legend of Merlin relates that Vortigern could not build his fastness until the foundation-stone was wetted with the blood of a child without a father.[329] So in Scotland there is a tradition that the Picts bathed the foundation stones of the prehistoric buildings which are called ' Picts' Houses ' with human blood.[330]

There are similar traditions in almost every land. Thus it is related that the walls of Copenhagen repeatedly sank as they were being built, until a little girl, seated in a chair beside a table loaded with playthings and sweetmeats, was built into the rampart. Then the walls stood firm.[331] So when the Castle of Liebenstein in Thuringia was built a child was bought from its mother and walled in. The little one was eating a cake as the masons worked, and he cried : ' Mother, I see thee still.' Later, as the wall rose around him, he said : ' Mother I see thee a little still.' As the last stone was put in, he cried : ' Mother, now I see thee no more ! ' [332] So in another part of Germany there was a tradition that a maiden had been built into the wall of the Castle of Nieder Manderscheid. The wall was broken through in 1844, at the point indicated by the legend, and a skeleton was found embedded in it.[333] Similarly, when the Bridge Gate at Bremen was demolished some years ago the skeleton of a child was found embedded in the foundations.[334] And so in several instances in our own land. Thus, when the parish church of Holsworthy in Devon was restored in 1885, a skeleton was found embedded in stone and mortar in the south-west wall. There was every indication of a burial alive. It is noticeable that this portion of the wall was faulty, and had settled. When the parish church of Wickenby in Lincolnshire was restored some years ago the complete skeleton of a man was found buried in the foundations of the west wall.[335] When the parish church at Brownsover, near Rugby, was restored in 1876 two skeletons were found, one under the north wall, and one under the south wall. The bodies had been placed in a small excavation in the clay, made for the purpose, and covered with slabs of oak, and the original foundation had been laid above.[336]

Sometimes a rationalizing legend has arisen to account for these wall burials. There are many of these : one may serve as a sample. A knight began to build himself a house (now known as Barn Hall, in the parish of Tolleshunt Knights, in Essex) but the Devil threw down every night what had been built during the day. So the knight watched all one night, caught the Devil in the act, and had a sharp tussle with him. The Evil One was so enraged that he swore that on the knight's death he would have him, whether he were buried in the church or out of it. When the brave knight's days were ended he was buried in the wall of the church, half in and half out, and the Devil was cheated.[337] Obviously this is a story made up to account for the finding of a body buried in the wall of a church.

Within historic times the custom has probably been carried out in Europe. Thus it is related that in 1615 Count Anthony Günther of Oldenburg, when visiting a dyke that was under construction, actually found the workmen about to bury a child beneath it. He saved the child, and imprisoned the mother who had sold it for the purpose.[338] In other parts of the world the memory survives vividly among the common people. There has been unrest among the native population during quite recent years in Singapore, Shanghai, and Calcutta, because the notion got abroad that human victims were wanted by the British authorities to be buried in the foundations of various buildings and bridges. Sometimes the human victim offered in earlier times is remembered by some association with the shadow or with the name of a man. Thus the Roumanians of Transylvania believe that if the mason lays the foundation-stone upon a man's shadow, the man will die within forty days, and anyone passing a building in course of erection may be warned, ' Beware lest they take thy shadow ! ' [339] And in Russia, where in some provinces an animal is killed and buried on the spot where the first log or the first stone is to be placed, and where, in other provinces, the builders call out instead the name of some bird or beast, believing that it will then rapidly die, it is significant that the peasants are very polite to the builders on the latter occasion, because their own names might be maliciously called out instead by the workmen if they were annoyed. [340]

Sometimes a puppet is substituted for a man in propitiatory rites, and perhaps this is an intermediate stage between the actual sacrifice of a man and the later usage by which an animal is sacrificed instead of a man, though there are many instances also in which an image is offered instead of the animal sacrifice that has become usual. [341] In many cases, however, the image definitely represents a man. So in relation to the striking tradition of the dedication of himself to death (*devotio*) on the part of a Roman commander as a sacrifice to assure victory (such a story is related of Decius Mus at the battle of Vesuvius in the third century before Christ, and later of his son and grandson), Livy tells us that a private soldier might be chosen by the general to represent him, and if this man were not killed in battle by the enemy ' an image of the man, seven feet high at least, must be buried in the earth ', and some other propitiatory rites performed.[342] Pausanias relates that the Phocians, in the course of a war with the Thessalians, prepared to kill their women and children and burn them on a funeral pyre, if defeated.   In the event they were victorious, but at the feast of the Elaphebolia in memory of the victory a pyre was always erected and set on fire, with figures in the shape of human beings laid upon it.   There appear to be survivals of such a custom in Greece to-day.[343]   The same substitution has come to pass with regard to sacrifices at foundations.   Thus in some English churches images have been found buried in the walls, as at Chulmleigh in Devon, where an early carved figure of Christ had been embedded in a wall, which, being defective, had been rebuilt in the fifteenth century.[344]

But generally the human sacrifice has become changed into that of an animal.   Thus Pausanias tells us that the people of Potniae, in earlier times, sacrificed a boy yearly to Dionysius, but the sacrifice had been commuted by his day for a goat.[345]   So lambs and buffaloes are now sacrificed to the earth-gods of some of the Dravidian tribes in India, as a substitute for the human sacrifices which were formerly offered.[346]   When an English officer put down human sacrifice among the Khonds of Orissa they at once began to discuss the possibility of sacrificing cattle instead.[347]   This, again, holds true of sacrifices offered in connexion with foundations. A dyke in Walcheren is called Hontsdamm because the workmen who repaired it in the twelfth century encountered a quicksand, and could not make the dyke firm until they buried a live dog beneath it.[348] Various animals used to be sacrificed on laying the foundation of a building in Ireland up to comparatively recent times.[349] As late as 1862 it was usual to smear the blood of a cock on the foundation of houses at Quimper.[350] A French savant actually saw the cock sacrificed and the blood poured out on the threshold about sixty years ago in Normandy.[351] In Borneo a slave-girl used to be flung into the hole prepared for the first pole of a house, and crushed to death when the post descended. Later on the rite was commuted for the sacrifice of a chicken.[352] Even when a substitution of this sort has been long effected there is often some distinct trace of the earlier human sacrifice. Thus in Greece to-day it is believed that the first passer-by after the foundation-stone is laid will die within the year unless a lamb or a cock is killed upon the stone.[353]

But it is naturally in relation to the building of bridges that there are the most vivid traces of the old rites. A bridge was more difficult and dangerous to build than a house ; it was much harder to secure good foundations ; and the bridge was much more liable to be swept away by floods than any other structure. When this last happened, what more natural than to suppose that the spirit of the river was angry, and had risen in wrath to destroy the daring work of men ? Apart from bridges altogether there is much evidence of human sacrifice to water-spirits. The Franks used to offer a sacrifice of women and children on crossing a river. In Timor a young girl was taken to the bank of the river and placed on a sacred stone from which she was presently dragged by the crocodiles.[354] On the Guinea coast a man was periodically taken out in a canoe, and thrown to the sharks, as a sacrifice to the sea.[355] Cicero says that Roman generals ' embarking on the sea, have been accustomed to sacrifice a victim to the waves '.[356] The Greek διαβατήρια was a similar sort of custom.[357] It meant a sacrifice on passing a border, but the border was almost always a river or the sea. In these last examples the victim was an animal, but in earlier days there had probably been a human sacrifice in both rites.

The reluctance to save a drowning man which has prevailed in many parts of the world belongs to this range of ideas. If you save a man who is drowning you rob the river or the sea of its victim, and probably you yourself will become the victim instead, for the angry spirit of the waters will not be balked of its prey.[358]

The same civilizing process of substituting puppets or animals for human beings that we have seen already in the case of the general practice of foundation-sacrifice, has also obtained in regard to sacrifices to rivers for the prevention of floods (or conversely, in Egypt, for the promotion of the fertilizing inundation of the Nile), or for the preservation of bridges. Sometimes it is a puppet that is substituted for a human being. The Pons Sublicius was the oldest bridge in Rome ; it was entirely of wood, and no iron or bronze were allowed to be used in the repair of it. Every year on the ides of May there was a solemn procession to the bridge of the magistrates, the pontifices, the Vestal Virgins, and the

Flaminica Dialis, who was in mourning garb. The
Vestals cast into the Tiber, from the bridge, twenty-
four puppets of straw, which were called Argei.
Plutarch says that the Argei were originally Greeks
who were flung into the river and drowned, and that
Hercules taught the Romans to throw in these
images instead.[359] There can scarcely be any doubt
that the custom is at any rate a remembrance of
human sacrifice. And so in Egypt. There was a
canal called the Khalig that ran from the Nile
through the centre of Cairo. Its mouth was closed
by a dam during the low Nile season. When the
Nile rose to a certain height the dam was cut.
' Tradition relates that in olden days a virgin wearing
costly jewels was on this occasion thrown into the
Khalig as a propitiatory offering to the god. . . .
In more enlightened times a doll was substituted
for the human sacrifice.' [360] Very often, again, an
animal is the substitute. The Pulians used to offer
a bull in sacrifice to the River Alpheios. Plutarch
tells us that Lucullus sacrificed a bull to the
Euphrates, on crossing the river with his army.[361]
In Russia a horse is flung into the river with a couple
of millstones fastened to its neck to appease the
Vodyany, the water spirit, in the early spring when
floods are rife.[362]

The next development, under the influence of
civilization and Christianity, is to think of the
animal, not as deliberately offered in sacrifice to the
spirits of the earth or the water, but as thrown to
the Devil to cheat him of human prey. This applies
to other buildings beside bridges. So the minster
at Aix-la-Chapelle was built by the aid of the
Devil, whose reward was to be whoever first crossed

the threshold when the church was completed.   A
chained wolf was loosed as the procession was about
to enter the building, and rushed through the door.
The Devil howled with rage, snatched up the wolf,
and kicked the door in spite as he departed.   The
split oak is shown to this day.³⁶³   There are bridges
all over Europe about which some such legend is
told, as, for example, at Aberystwyth in Wales, at
Frankfort in Germany, at Cahors in France, and in
the St. Gothard pass in Switzerland.   Usually the
bridge has been completed, after repeated failures
on the part of the builders, by the aid of the Devil,
who bargains for the first living thing that crosses
the bridge as his reward.   Then a dog (as at the
Devil's Bridge over the Reuss) or a cock (as at the
Sachsenhausen Bridge at Frankfort) is driven
across, and the Devil is cheated.³⁶⁴

It is probably this later legendary association
with the Devil that accounts for the eschatological
character of some of the foreign games of the type
of *London Bridge is Broken Down*, where the bridge-
keepers, who make the arch with their arms, are
called ' The Devil and the Angel ', or ' St. Peter and
St. Paul ' ;   and where the game itself is called
Heaven and Hell, as in France, or *Open the Gates*, as
in Italy, the portals being those of heaven and hell.
In the French game the children who have chosen
the right side, at the finish of the game, pursue those
who have chosen the other side, with the fingers
extended from the forehead to imitate devils' horns.

But there are ample traces of the original human
sacrifice in European legend.   Thus in Italy the
bridge of Arta kept falling down until they walled
in the wife of the master-mason, and with her last

breath she laid a curse upon the bridge that for all time it should tremble like a flower-stalk.[365]   And so in France.   When the bridge of Rosporden in Brittany was being built it fell down repeatedly, and finally it was decided that it was necessary to immure a victim.   A little boy of four years old was built in, with a candle in one hand, and a piece of bread in the other, and when the wind howls at night you can hear him crying :

> ' Ma chandelle est morte, ma mère,
> Et de pain, il ne m'en reste guère.'[366]
>
> (' My candle has gone out, O mother mine,
> My bread is nearly done, and I shall pine ! ')

There was a story current among the peasantry in Warwickshire, thirty years ago, that the bridge in Stoneleigh Park had one or more human victims immured in the foundations.   Now some versions of the rhyme *London Bridge is Broken Down* have the refrain :

> ' Dance over my lady Lee ! '

—and there has been an attempt to connect this name with the noble family of Leigh, whose seat is at Stoneleigh, and with the fact that an ancestor of the family was Sir Thomas Leigh, who was Lord Mayor of London in 1558.   We should suggest that it is precisely the other way round—that the existence of ' Lady Lee ' in the refrain (is there any connexion with the River Lea which is a tributary of the Thames ?) has given rise to the legend about the Leighs and Stoneleigh.

But there can be no doubt that when children

play at the game of *London Bridge is Broken Down*, or any of its analogues, they are unconsciously preserving the memory of the dark rite by which a human being was originally sacrificed to secure the stability of a bridge.

NOTES

1. *Odyssey*, VI, 99–101.
2. *Tristia*, III, *Eleg.* 12.
3. *Odes*, III, 24.
4. *Anth. Graec.*, VII, 89.
5. *Aeneid*, VII, 378–379.
6. *Satyricon*, 64. The parallel is pointed out by Tylor, *Primitive Culture*, I, p. 67.
7. So in Germany, where one series is : ' Kaiser, König, Eddelmann, Bürger, Bauer, Beddelmann.' Simrock, *Das deutsche Kinderbuch*, p. 218.
8. Cf. Maclagan, *Games and Diversions of Argyleshire*, p. 5.
9. Walther von der Vogelweide (ed. Pfeiffer), p. 51.
10. *Faust*, I, 2826–2829.
11. *Gargantua* (ed. H. Clouzot), pp. 78–80.
12. Salzman, *English Life in the Middle Ages*, p. 99.
13. *Hamlet*, III, 4, 76–77.
14. *All's Well that Ends Well*, IV, 3, 136.
15. Hone, *Table Book*, p. 39.
16. *Hesperides*, p. 29.
17. Seebohm, *The English Village Community*, p. 3.
18. Seebohm, *Customary Acres and Their Historical Importance*, pp. vii and 101.
19. Barnabe Googe, *The Popish Kingdome*, p. 63.
20. *Gentleman's Magazine* (1809), I, p. 33.
21. Brand, *Popular Antiquities*, I, p. 119. Cf. Herrick, *Hesperides*, p. 19.
22. Hone, *The Year Book*, p. 1179. *Gentleman's Magazine* (1833), I, p. 117.
23. Brand, *Popular Antiquities*, I, p. 139.
24. Lady Gomme, *Traditional Games*, II, pp. 122–123.
25. Stewart Culin, *Games of the North American Indians*, p. 34.
26. Matt. xi. 16–17.
27. Newell, *Games and Songs of American Children*, pp. 381–382.
28. *Ibid.*, pp. 383–384.
29. *Ibid.*, pp. 376–378. Lady Gomme, *Traditional Games*, II, pp. 176–178.
30. An old woman in the High Peak of Derbyshire recited to an inquirer a version in which after the words ' Pray, young lady come out of the water ', the players ducked

9

under the arms of the leaders and said : ' Dig under th' water-hole '.—*Notes and Queries*, (Ninth Series) XII, p. 474.

31. Eckenstein, *Comparative Studies in Nursery Rhymes*, pp. 75–76.

32. This custom confirms Mr. Jevons's suggestion (in his Introduction to Philemon Holland's translation of Plutarch's *Romane Questions*, p. 101) that in the Roman usage the sprinkling with water was ' originally an introduction of the strange woman to the local water-spirit '. So among the Bakitara, after the first meal which the bride has cooked has been eaten, she goes to the well and brings back water and some sticks for the fire, and this is regarded as completing the marriage ceremony.—Roscoe, *The Bakitara*, p. 280.

33. Frazer, *Totemism and Exogamy*, I, p. 33.

34. Hutchinson, *Marriage Customs*, pp. 80, 184, 201. Cf. Westermarck, *Marriage Ceremonies in Morocco*, p. 198.

35. Celnart, *Nouveau manuel complet des Jeux de Société*, pp. 3–4. Rolland, *Rimes et Jeux de l'Enfance*, pp. 78–79.

36. Celnart, *Nouveau manuel complet des Jeux de Société*, p. 4.

37. Lady Gomme, *Traditional Games*, I, pp. 4–5.

38. Hone, *Every Day Book*, II, p. 666.

39. Newell, *Games and Songs of American Children*, p. 385.

40. Judges xxi. 6–23.

41. Ἐγάμουν δὲ δι' ἁρπαγῆς, οὐ μικρὰς οὐδὲ ἀώρους πρὸς γάμον, ἀλλα καὶ ἀκμαζούσας καὶ πεπείρους.—*Life of Lycurgus*, XV, 35. It looks as if there is a trace of the survival of this custom in Greece, many centuries later, in a poem by Palladas of Alexandria in the Greek Anthology (VII, 610), where ' one *carried off* (ἥρπασε) the bride '.

42. ' A totemic clan is usually also exogamous. But to this rule there are very considerable exceptions.'—Frazer, *Totemism and Exogamy*, IV, p. 8.

43. Westermarck, *History of Human Marriage*, II, p. 105.

44. *Ibid.*, p. 115, Dr. Westermarck says that there are five hundred and thirty family names in China.

45. Tylor, *Early History of Mankind*, p. 280.

46. Lord Avebury, *The Origin of Civilisation*, p. 98.

47. Tylor, *Early History of Mankind*, p. 280.

48. Lord Avebury, *The Origin of Civilisation*, pp. 96–97.

49. Theal, *Kaffir Folk Lore*, p. 210.

50. Hartland, *Primitive Law*, p. 165. Cf. Westermarck, *History of Human Marriage*, II, p. 123.

51. Tylor, *Early History of Mankind*, p. 281.

52. *Ibid.*, p. 287.

53. Westermarck, *History of Human Marriage*, II, p. 246.

54. McLennan, *Primitive Marriage*, p. 21.

55. Frazer, *Totemism and Exogamy*, III, p. 582.

56. McLennan, *Primitive Marriage*, pp. 39–40.

57. *Ibid.*, p. 25.

58. Westermarck, *History of Human Marriage*, II, p. 265. In ancient Rome the bride's girdle was tied in the *nodus Herculaneus*—a difficult knot which the bridegroom had to unloose in bed.

59. Tylor, *Early History of Mankind*, p. 287.

60. Westermarck, *History of Human Marriage*, II, p. 268.

61. *Gentleman's Magazine*, (1767) p. 140, (1770) p. 137.

62. Brand, *Popular Antiquities*, II, p. 96. Lady Wilde, *Ancient Legends of Ireland*, p. 115.

63. Brand, *Popular Antiquities*, II, p. 87.

64. *History of Man*, II, p. 59. Cf. Roberts, *The Cambrian Popular Antiquities*, pp. 162–164.

65. McLennan, *Primitive Marriage*, p. 21.

66. *Ibid.*, p. 56.

67. *Notes and Queries* (First Series) II, p. 196 ; VII, p. 28.

68. Tennyson, *Lyrical Monologue*.

69. Tylor, *Primitive Culture*, I, p. 73. Lord Avebury, *The Origin of Civilisation*, p. 74.

70. Westermarck, *Marriage Ceremonies in Morocco*, pp. 163, 325, 334.

71. *Ibid.*, p. 326.

72. Sir J. G. Frazer, *Folklore in the Old Testament*, III, pp. 10–11, pronounces against the connexion of bride-lifting with marriage by capture, and attributes the custom solely to the sanctity of the threshold, mainly on the ground ' that the custom of lifting the bride over the threshold can hardly be separated from the custom which enjoins the bride to step over the threshold without touching it ', in which latter usage ' there is no suggestion of violence or constraint '. Compare Westermarck, *History of Human Marriage*, II, p. 277 ; and, on the other side, Lord Avebury, *The Origin of Civilisation*, pp. 60, 84, and Mr. Jevons's Introduction to Philemon Holland's translation of Plutarch's *Romane Questions*, pp. 32, 96.

73. Westermarck, *History of Human Marriage*, II, p. 536.

74. A reference to the custom in ancient Rome by which the bride on arrival at her future home smeared the door-posts with wolf's fat and oil, and wound fillets of wool

around them, after which she was carried over the threshold. See W. Warde Fowler, *The Religious Experience of the Roman People*, p. 83.

75. Once a common custom in England. See *Notes and Queries*, (Fourth Series) XII, p. 468, and many other places. Cf. Hunt, *Popular Romances of the West of England*, p. 379.

76. In the *Letters on Demonology and Witchcraft*, p. 83, Scott again mentions bride-lifting as common in the south of Scotland. In this place he adds that ' the custom was universal in Rome, where it was observed as keeping in memory the rape of the Sabines, and that it was by a show of violence toward the females that the object of peopling the city was attained '.

77. Thus anything fast would interfere with the freedom of the escaping soul. So it was believed in the Isle of Man that the ghost of a dead man would walk unless the knots in the shroud were undone before burial, and a case is recorded in which the grave was actually opened, the day after the funeral, to do this when it had been overlooked. *Notes and Queries*, (Third Series) III, p. 443. The same superstition existed in Germany and Switzerland. Frazer, *The Golden Bough*, I, p. 401. (I may remark here that the numerous references to *The Golden Bough* which occur later in these notes are all to the second (revised and enlarged) edition of 1900, except where otherwise stated).

78. So the common knot-grass was thought to have the power of checking growth in children. Lysander, alluding to her small stature, says to Hermia in the *Midsummer Night's Dream*, III, 2, 329–331 :

' Get you gone, you dwarf ;
You minimus, of hindering knot-grass made ;
You bead, you acorn ! '

79. Frazer, *The Golden Bough*, I, p. 392 sqq. Abbott, *Macedonian Folklore*, p. 100.

80. Plutarch, *Quaest. Roman.*, Q. 27. W. Warde Fowler, *The Religious Experience of the Roman People*, p. 214.

81. Frazer, *Folk-Lore in the Old Testament*, III, p. 3.

82. Lean, *Collectanea*, II, p. 73.

83. In some parts of Yorkshire a kettle-full of hot water was poured over the threshold after the bride had gone, ' to keep it warm for the next bride '.—*Notes and Queries*, (Second Series) XII, p. 490.

84. Brand, *Popular Antiquities*, III, pp. 133–134.
85. Merivale, *History of the Romans under the Empire*, II, p. 447.
86. Thierry, *Norman Conquest*, I, p. 159.
87. A. G. Tansley, *The New Psychology*, p. 129.
88. Plutarch, *Quaest. Roman.*, Q. 29.
89. McLennan, *Primitive Marriage*, p. 25.
90. Tremearne, *Hausa Superstitions and Customs*, p. 86.
91. Tylor, *Early History of Mankind*, p. 287.
92. Lady Gomme, *Traditional Games*, I, pp. 109, 305; II, p. 100.
93. Westermarck, *Marriage Ceremonies in Morocco*, p. 165.
94. Grimm, *Household Tales*, I, p. 271.
95. Macculloch, *The Childhood of Fiction*, pp. 20–21.

96.   ' We come to see Genesis, Genesis, Genesis,
    We come to see Genesis ; how is she to-day ? '—

    R. C. Maclagan, *The Games and Diversions of Argyleshire*, p. 123.
    It is related of *Genesis* in the course of the game that ' she fell down the stairs and broke her big toe ! '
97. It is *Janet jo* generally in Scotland. Chambers, *Popular Rhymes of Scotland*, p. 140.
98. A version has been recorded in Dublin which has the lines :

    ' Black is for the Devil, and that won't do '.
    ' O white is for the angels, and that will do '.

    —*Notes and Queries*, (Twelfth Series) VIII, p. 176.
    White, it will be remembered, was the mourning colour in ancient Rome.—Plutarch, *Quaest. Roman.*, 26.
99. Lady Gomme, *Traditional Games*, I, pp. 271–272.
100. Dole—lamentation. So often in Shakespeare. ' What dreadful dole is here ! ' (*Midsummer-Night's Dream*, V, I, 283). ' The poor old man, their father, making such pitiful dole over them that all the beholders take his part with weeping ' (*As You Like It*, I, 2, 139).
101. Lady Gomme, *Traditional Games*, I, p. 43.
102. Rolland, *Rimes et Jeux de l'Enfance*, p. 191.
103. W. Warde Fowler, *The Roman Festivals*, p. 308.
104. *Aeneid*, V, 79–80.
105. In some places custom ordained that there should be nine leaves in the sprig of oak that was worn.—*Notes and Queries*, (5th Series) X, p. 494.
106. It is said it was a common custom in the south of Ireland for boys to run about stinging people with bunches of nettles on the occasion of the Beltane fire on the eve of May.—Hone, *Every Day Book*, I, p. 594.

107. Tennyson, *The Talking Oak*.
108. Newell, *Games and Songs of American Children*, pp. 113–114.
109. *The Life of Gargantua*, p. 70.
110. Newell, *Games and Songs of American Children*, p. 114.
111. This is a noteworthy detail, for in very many cases the leaf-clad person in the spring rites which we shall afterwards describe is drenched with water—a usage that is still found in Europe as a rain-charm.—Frazer, *The Golden Bough*, II, p. 121.
112. Sebillot, *Le Folk Lore de France*, III, p. 525.
113. See Brand, *Popular Antiquities*, I, pp. 125–143. Frazer, *The Golden Bough*, I, pp. 193–224.
114. W. Warde Fowler, *The Roman Festivals*, pp. 91–94.
115. Caesar, *De Bello Gallico*, VI, 16. Frazer, *The Golden Bough*, III, p. 320.
116. *Ibid.*, II, p. 62.
117. *Ibid.*, II, p. 60.
118. *Ibid.*, II, p. 63.
119. *Ibid.*, II, pp. 79, 93.
120. *Ibid.*, II, pp. 84, 91. Cf. Brand, *Popular Antiquities*, I, pp. 127, 138. Grimm, *Teutonic Mythology*, II, pp. 764–768.
121. Frazer, *The Golden Bough*, II, p. 82.
122. Olaus Magnus, *A Compendious History of the Goths, Swedes, and Vandals* (1658), p. 166.
123. The comparison was frequent. So when Hermia is rating Helena, in the *Midsummer-Night's Dream* (III, 2) she says:

    ' How low am I, thou painted maypole ? speak ;
    How low am I ? '

124. Stow, *Survey of London*, p. 130.
125. Gardiner, *History of England*, VII, p. 321.
126. Brand, *Popular Antiquities*, I, p. 140.
127. *Ibid.*, I, p. 135. Stubbs, *Anatomie of Abuses*, p. 94.
128. Napier, *Folk Lore of the West of Scotland*, p. 79.
129. Frazer, *The Golden Bough*, I, p. 193.
130. W. Warde Fowler, *The Roman Festivals*, p. 80.
131. Frazer, *The Golden Bough*, I, p. 197.
132. Sops-in-wine were a kind of pinks.
133. As to the whitethorn see Brand, *Popular Antiquities*, I, p. 131.
134. In the *Midsummer Night's Dream*, IV, 1, 131–132, when the lovers are found asleep in the forest, Theseus says :

    ' No doubt they rose up early to observe
    The rite of May.'

So in *Henry VIII*, V, 4, 14-15 :

> ' 'Tis as much impossible . . .
> To scatter 'em, as 'tis to make 'em sleep
> On May-day morning.'

135. Stubbs, *Anatomie of Abuses*, p. 94. Brand, *Popular Antiquities*, I, p. 129.
136. Salzman, *English Life in the Middle Ages*, p. 84.
137. *Notes and Queries*, (Eleventh Series) XII., p. 74.
138. Newell, *English Folk Rhymes*, pp. 238-239.
139. Nilsson, *A History of Greek Religion*, p. 93.
140. Brand, *Popular Antiquities*, I, p. 131.
141. The inn sign of ' The Green Man ' is derived from this custom.
142. Hone, *Every Day Book*, II, p. 577.
143. J. B. Firth, *Highways and Byways in Derbyshire*, p. 223.
144. Brand, *Popular Antiquities*, I, p. 57. Hone, *Every Day Book*, I, p. 252.
145. *Merry Wives of Windsor*, V, 5, 137.
146. Jonathan Couch, *History of Polperro*, p. 152.
147. *Notes and Queries*, (Second Series) II, p. 405 ; (Sixth Series) III, p. 386.
148. Lady Gomme, *Traditional Games*, I, pp. 233-235. Northall, *English Folk Rhymes*, pp. 396-398.
149. Northall, *English Folk Rhymes*, p. 397.
150. Newell, *Games and Songs of American Children*, p. 91.
151. Lady Gomme, *Traditional Games*, II, p. 178.
152. Hone, *The Year Book*, p. 1595.
153. Lang, *Myth, Ritual, and Religion*, I, p. 282.
154. Gilbert Murray, *Five Stages of Greek Religion*, p. 44.
155. W. Warde Fowler, *The Religious Experience of the Roman People*, pp. 96-97, 103. Frazer, *The Golden Bough*, III, pp. 123-124.
156. Hunt, *Popular Romances of the West of England*, p. 383.
157. F. H. Kidson and Mary Neal, *English Folk-Song and Dance*, p. 150.
158. *Gentleman's Magazine*, 1790, p. 520.
159. The same correspondent later on recollected several lines of the song :

> ' Robin Hood and Little John
> They are both gone to the fair O !
> And we will go to the merry greenwood
> To see what they do there O !

And cheerily we'll get up
As soon as any day O !
All for to bring the summer home,
The Summer and the May O ! '
—*Gentleman's Magazine*, 1790, II, p. 1100

160. Brand, *Popular Antiquities*, I, p. 133.
161. Lady Gomme, *Traditional Games*, II, pp. 207, 386–387.
162. Kidson and Neal, *English Folk-Song and Dance*, p. 105.
163. Brand, *Popular Antiquities*, I, pp. 158–159.
164. Hone, *Every Day Book*, I, p. 431.
165. Northall, *English Folk Rhymes*, pp. 192–1923.
166. *Itinerary through Wales*, II, pp. 29–30.
167. Northall, *English Folk Rhymes*, pp. 370–371. Lady Gomme, *Traditional Games*, II, pp. 3–13. Newell, *Games and Songs of American Children*, pp. 80–84. The game was recorded in Lincolnshire forty years ago with the formula :

' A-waiting fur a pardner,
A-waiting fur a pardner,
You an' I an' ivryone knows
How whoats an' beans an' barley grows '.

Then the imitative action followed, in the usual way.
—*Notes and Queries*, (Seventh Series) XII, p. 493.
168. Rolland, *Rimes et Jeux de l'Enfance*, pp. 99–100.
169. Tylor, *Primitive Culture*, I, p. 130. Grimm, *Teutonic Mythology*, pp. 713–715.
170. Frazer, *The Golden Bough*, I, pp. 45–47.
171. *Henry V*, II, 3.
172. Newell, *Games and Songs of American Children*, p. 84.
173. *Gentleman's Magazine*, 1822, I, p. 14.
174. Frazer, *The Golden Bough*, I, p. 36.
175. *Ibid.*, I, pp. 137–139.
176. *Ibid.*, II, pp. 27–29.
177. A great deal of evidence about swinging is collected by Sir J. G. Frazer in an appendix to *The Golden Bough* (2nd ed.), II, pp. 449–456. See also pp. 343–344.
178. W. Warde Fowler, *The Religious Experience of the Roman People*, pp. 61–67.
179. *Georgics*, II, 388–389.
180. *De Incarnatione Verbi*, I, 25.
181. *Notes and Queries*, (First Series) XI, p. 397.
182. Northall, *English Folk Rhymes*, p. 245.

183. Chambers, *Popular Rhymes of Scotland*, p. 154.
184. But at Clifton, near Nottingham, the children say :

> ' Please to remember the fifth of November
> Old Guy Fawkes and Gunpowder Plot
> Shall never be forgot,
> While Nottingham Castle stands on a rock.'
> —Northall, *English Folk Rhymes*, p. 245.

185. *Ibid.*, p. 248.
186. Gardiner, *History of England*, I, p. 286.
187. Brand, *Popular Antiquities*, I, p. 14. Hone, *Every Day Book*, I, p. 58. Frazer, *The Golden Bough*, III, p. 238. *Ibid.*, (*Balder the Beautiful*), I, p. 107.
188. M. A. Murray, *The Witch Cult in Western Europe*, p. 109.
189. Frazer, *The Golden Bough*, pp. 244, 256, 268.
190. Brand, *Popular Antiquities*, I, pp. 167, 174. Hunt, *Popular Romances of the West of England*, p. 207.
191. *Monthly Chronicle of North Country Lore and Legend* (1887), p. 405.
192. *Notes and Queries*, (Third Series) XII, p. 42.
193. The Cretan Spring-song of the Kouretes prays for νέοι πολῖται among the other gifts of the spring. Gilbert Murray, *Five Stages of Greek Religion*, p. 46.
194. *Moralia* (ed. King), p. 45.
195. Frazer, *The Magical Origin of Kings*, pp. 101–102.
196. Tylor, *Primitive Culture*, II, p. 298.
197. Frazer, *The Golden Bough* (1922), p. 633-634.
198. Brand, *Popular Antiquities*, p. 127. Hone, *Every Day Book*, II, p. 848. Scott, *Demonology and Witchcraft*, p. 78.
199. Pennant, *Scottish Tours*, I, p. 111. Scott, *Demonology and Witchcraft*, p. 78.
200. May Day was called in Irish Lá-Beltaine.—Lady Wilde *Ancient Legends of Ireland*, p. 102.
201. Frazer, *The Golden Bough*, III, pp. 261–262.
202. J. Napier, *Folk Lore of the West of Scotland*, p. 168. Hone, *Every Day Book*, II, p. 659. Frazer, *The Golden Bough*, III, p. 263. *Ibid.*, (*Balder the Beautiful*), II, p. 25.
203. Similarly there was a pretence of burning the man clad in green and called ' The Green Wolf ' at Jumièges in Normandy in the midsummer fire.—Frazer, *The Golden Bough* (*Balder the Beautiful*), I, pp. 185–186 ; II, p. 25.
204. Brand, *Popular Antiquities*, I, p. 166.
205. Frazer, *The Golden Bough* (*Balder the Beautiful*), I, pp. 117–118, 143, 164.
206. Barnabe Googe, *The Popish Kingdome*, p. 54.

207. Clodd, *Tom-Tit-Tot*, p. 34.
208. For the Sword-Dance generally, see Chambers, *The Mediaeval Stage*, I, pp. 182–227 ; II, p. 270.
209. Olaus Magnus, *A Compendious History of the Goths, Swedes, and Vandals* (1658), pp. 167–168.
210. Brand, *Popular Antiquities*, I, p. 283.
211. Hunt, *Popular Romances of the West of England*, p. 390.
212. Chambers, *Popular Rhymes of Scotland*, p. 169.
213. *Gentleman's Magazine* (1811), p. 422.
214. Hone, *Every Day Book*, pp. 1645–1648.
215. Hunt, *Popular Romances of the West of England*, pp. 391–392.
216. A keelman was a boatman on the Tyne, engaged on the boats which carried coal and were known as ' keels ', as in the song : ' Weel may the keelie row that my laddie's in ! '
217. *Monthly Chronicle of North Country Lore and Legend* (1887), 462–465.
218. Frazer, *The Golden Bough*, II, p. 62.
219. Lord Avebury, *The Origin of Civilisation*, p. 212.
220. Lev. vi. 13.
221. Frazer, *The Golden Bough*, I, p. 168 ; III, p. 252.
222. W. Warde Fowler, *The Roman Festivals*, p. 147.
223. Prescott, *The Conquest of Peru*, I, p. 99.
224. Tylor, *Primitive Culture*, I, p. 76. Northall, *English Folk Rhymes*, p. 405.
225. Grimm, *Teutonic Mythology*, II, p. 853.
226. Frazer, *The Golden Bough*, III, p. 348.
227. *Ibid.*, (*Spirits of the Corn and the Wild*), II, p. 314.
228. Count G. d'Alviella, *The Origin and Growth of the Conception of God*, p. 37.
229. Frazer, *The Golden Bough*, III, pp. 276, 348.
230. *The Golden Bough* (*Balder the Beautiful*), I, pp. 147–156.
231. Stewart Culin, *Games of the North American Indians*, p. 733.
232. *Gentleman's Magazine*, 1738, p. 80. *Notes and Queries*, (Tenth Series) VI, p. 476.
233. Newell, *Games and Songs of American Children*, pp. 275–276.
234. Simrock, *Das deutsche Kinderbuch*, p. 237.
235. *Notes and Queries*, (Eleventh Series) VIII, p. 34.
236. A. Birlinger, *Nimm mich mit! Kinderbüchlein*, pp. 129–130.
237. Kirk, *A Secret Commonwealth of Elves*, p. 6.
238. Grimm. *Teutonic Mythology*, II, pp. 515–516, Dasent, *Popular Tales from the Norse*, p. 74.

239. Grimm, *Teutonic Mythology*, II, p. 449.
240. Hartland, *The Science of Fairy Tales*, p. 105.
241. *Ibid.*, p. 167.
242. *Ibid.*, p. 113.
243. Reginald Scot, *Discoverie of Witchcraft*, II, c. 4.
244. Grimm, *Household Tales*, II, p. 56.
245. Macculloch, *The Childhood of Fiction*, p. 44.
246. Grimm, *Teutonic Mythology*, II, p. 454.
247. Rhys, *Celtic Folklore*, I, p. 8 ; II, pp. 418–419.
248. Grimm, *Teutonic Mythology*, II, p. 461.
249. Hartland, *The Science of Fairy Tales*, p. 50.
250. Grimm, *Teutonic Mythology*, II, p. 459.
251. Hunt, *Popular Romances of the West of England*, p. 81.
252. Keightley, *The Fairy Mythology*, p. 298.
253. *Ibid.*, p. 164.
254. Hunt, *Popular Romances of the West of England*, p. 349.
255. Keightley, *The Fairy Mythology*, p. 112.
256. Grimm, *Teutonic Mythology*, II, p. 494.
257. The same belief used to prevail in England and in Scotland.—Henderson, *The Folk Lore of the Northern Counties of England*, p. 149. Scott, *Demonology and Witchcraft*, p. 137.
258. *Notes and Queries*, (Sixth Series) VIII, p. 225. Cf. Frazer, *The Golden Bough (Balder the Beautiful)*, I, p. 15.
259. Tylor, *Primitive Culture*, I, p. 140. Lane, *Modern Egyptians*, p. 204.
260. Parker, *Village Folk Tales of Ceylon*, I, p. 137.
261. Pearson, *The Chances of Death*, II, p. 35.
262. Campbell, *Superstitions of the Scottish Highlands*, p. 153.
263. Hartland, *The Science of Fairy Tales*, p. 126.
264. *Ibid.*, p. 131.
265. Hunt, *Popular Romances of the West of England*, p. 238.
266. Hartland, *The Science of Fairy Tales*, p. 163.
267. *Ibid.*, p. 308.
268. *Ibid.*, p. 164.
269. Rhys, *Celtic Folklore*, I, pp. 35, 40, 46, 70 ; II, p. 583.
270. Northall, *English Folk Rhymes*, p. 407. Lady Gomme, *Traditional Games*, I, p. 48.
271. Simrock, *Das deutsche Kinderbuch*, p. 233.
272. *Ibid.*, p. 240.
273. Newell, *Games and Songs of American Children*, p. 137.
274. *Ibid.*, pp. 134–135.
275. Simrock, *Das deutsche Kinderbuch*, p. 241.
276. Lady Gomme, *Traditional Games*, II, p. 109.
277. Tylor, *Primitive Culture*, I, p. 98.

278. *Anth. Graec.*, XI, 268.
279. Abbott, *Macedonian Folklore*, p. 114.
280. *The Golden Legend*, f. XXI, B.
281. *Homilies* (ed. Griffiths), p. 227.
282. *Notes and Queries*, (Sixth Series) IV, p. 27.
283. Frazer, *The Golden Bough*, II, p. 12.
284. Tremearne, *Hausa Superstitions and Customs*, p. 141.
285. Frazer, *The Golden Bough*, I, p. 279.
286. *Ibid.*, I, p. 256.
287. *Ibid.*, I, p. 313.
288. *Odyssey*, XVII, 541.
289. Abbott, *Macedonian Folk Lore*, p. 100.
290. *Anabasis*, II, 1, 5. Grote, *History of Greece*, VIII, p. 383.
291. *Notes and Queries*, (Sixth Series) I, p. 42.
292. *Anth. Graec.*, XI, 375.
293. Northall, *English Folk Rhymes*, p. 176.
294. *De doct. christ.*, II, 20. Cf. St. Thomas Aquinas, *Summa Theol.*, II, 2, qu. 96, art. 3.
295. Tylor, *Early History of Mankind*, p. 295.
296. Webster, *Basque Legends*, p. 73.
297. *Notes and Queries*, (First Series) XII, p. 200.
298. Tremearne, *Hausa Superstitions and Customs*, p. 532.
299. 2 Kings iv. 35.
300. See W. Warde Fowler, *The Roman Festivals*, pp. 314–315, and *The Religious Experience of the Roman People*, p. 112.
301. Pausanias, *Description of Greece*, IX, 39 (ed. Frazer), I, p. 495. Cf. Harrison, *Prolegomena to the Study of Greek Religion*, pp. 579–580.
302. Napier, *Folk Lore of the West of Scotland*, p. 41.
303. Lady Wilde, *Ancient Legends of Ireland*, I, p. 70.
304. Macculloch, *The Childhood of Fiction*, p. 290.
305. Grimm, *Household Tales*, I, p. 163.
306. Grimm, *Teutonic Mythology*, II, p. 502.
307. Dasent, *Popular Tales from the Norse*, p. 127.
308. Hartland, *The Science of Fairy Tales*, p. 113.
309. Rhys, *Celtic Folklore*, I, pp. 264–268.
310. Hartland, *The Science of Fairy Tales*, p. 116. The besom-maker who is the first interlocutor in a nonsense tale recorded in Germany is called ' Pif-paf-poltrie '.— Grimm, *Household Tales*, II, p. 176.
311. Macdougall, *Folk Tales and Fairy Lore*, pp. 102–103. Compare a story on p. 157.
312. Hartland, *The Science of Fairy Tales*, pp. 280–281.
313. Tylor, *Primitive Culture*, I, pp. 98, 103.
314. Hartland, *The Science of Fairy Tales*, 122–123.

315. *Ibid.*, pp. 245-246.
316. Hartland, *English Folk and Fairy Tales*, p. 143.
317. Northall, *English Folk Rhymes*, pp. 365-366. Lady Gomme, *Traditional Games*, II, pp. 441-442. Newell, *Games and Songs of American Children*, pp. 204-210.
318. Maclagan, *The Games and Diversions of Argyleshire*, pp. 237-238.
319. Newell, *Games and Songs of American Children*, p. 205.
320. *Gargantua*, p. 80. Zingerle, *Das deutsche Kinderspiel im Mittelalter*, p. 40, points out that the game is mentioned in the Middle Ages in Germany by Meister Altswert—' zwei spilten der fuln brucken '—and is also alluded to by Geiler von Keiserberg.
321. Mannhardt, *Das Brückenspiel*, in *Zeitschrift für deutsche Mythologie und Sittenkunde*, IV, pp. 302-309. Simrock, *Das deutsche Kinderbuch*, p. 25.
322. Celnart, *Nouveau manuel complet des Jeux de Société*, pp. 36-37.
323. Rolland, *Rimes et Jeux de l'Enfance*, pp. 141-142.
324. Celnart, *Nouveau manuel complet des Jeux de Société*, pp. 324-325.
325. Dumersan, *Chansons et Rondes Enfantines*, pp. 49-50.
326. Mannhardt, *Das Brückenspiel*, in *Zeitschrift für deutsche Mythologie und Sittenkunde*, IV, p. 302.
327. Tylor, *Primitive Culture*, I, p. 107.
328. Gomme, *Folk Lore Relics of Early Village Life*, p. 28.
329. Nennius, *Historia Britonum*, 39-42.
330. *Primitive Culture*, I, p. 104.
331. Baring Gould, *Strange Survivals*, p. 4.
332. Tylor, *Primitive Culture*, I, p. 105.
333. Baring Gould, *Strange Survivals*, p. 14.
334. *Ibid.*, p. 5.
335. *Ibid.*, pp. 13, 35.
336. Gomme, *Folk Lore Relics of Early Village Life*, p. 35.
337. *Ibid.*, p. 42.
338. Baring Gould, *Strange Survivals*, p. 15.
339. Frazer, *The Golden Bough*, I, p. 292.
340. Ralston, *Songs of the Russian People*, pp. 126-127.
341. In the early Aegean world the bull was frequently offered in effigy. Bulls of painted clay were manufactured for the use of the worshippers. The potters had moulds for producing them in large quantities.—Glotz, *The Aegean Civilisation*, p. 269. So images of oxen made of barley dough (ἐκ μάζης) were offered to Demeter ' that the real oxen might live '.—*Anth. Graec.*, VI., 40.

342. Livy, *History of Rome*, VIII, 10. Cf. W. Warde Fowler, *The Religious Experience of the Roman People*, pp. 206–208.

343. Nilsson, *A History of Greek Religion*, pp. 63, 90.

344. Baring Gould, *Strange Survivals*, p. 21. So also at Marton Church in Lincolnshire, where the image is now to be seen in the chancel.—Rawnsley, *Highways and Byways of Lincolnshire*, p. 139.

345. Lang, *Myth, Ritual, and Religion*, I, p. 271.

346. Frazer, *The Worship of Nature*, I, pp. 386–387.

347. Tylor, *Primitive Culture*, II, p. 405.

348. Baring Gould, *Strange Survivals*, p. 16.

349. Gomme, *Folk Lore Relics of Early Village Life*, p. 76.

350. Sebillot, *Le Folk Lore de France*, IV, p. 91.

351. Gomme, *Folk Lore Relics of Early Village Life*, p. 26.

352. Tylor, *Primitive Culture*, I, p. 107.

353. *Ibid.*, p. 106.

354. Tremearne, *Hausa Superstitions and Customs*, p. 136.

355. Tylor, *Primitive Culture*, II, p. 276.

356. Nostri quidem duces mare ingredientes immolare hostiam fluctibus consuerunt.—*De natura Deorum*, III, 20 (ed Mayor, III, p. 24).

357. Thucydides, V, 54.

358. Tylor, *Primitive Culture*, I, p. 108.

359. Plutarch, *Quaest. Roman.*, 32. Cf. W. Warde Fowler, *The Roman Festivals*, pp. 111–120.

360. Sir J. Rennell Rodd, *Social and Diplomatic Memories*, II, p. 84.

361. Plutarch, *Lives*, II, p. 222.

362. Tylor, *Primitive Culture*, II, p. 407.

363. Baring Gould, *Strange Survivals*, pp. 2–3.

364. There is a curious inversion of this in the Italian folk-sale of *The Penance of San Giuliano.*—See R. H. Busk, *The Folk Lore of Rome*, p. 207.

365. Tylor, *Primitive Culture*, I, p. 105.

366. Sebillot, *Le Folk Lore de France*, IV, pp. 89–90.

INDEX